POEMS

FROM A

GREEN & BLUE

PLANET

EDITED BY

SABRINA MAHFOUZ

HODDER CHILDREN'S BOOKS

First published in Great Britain in 2019 by Hodder & Stoughton

1 3 5 7 9 10 8 6 4 2

This collection copyright © Hodder Children's Books, 2019
All poems copyright © the individual poets
Introduction © Sabrina Mahfouz, 2019
Illustrations © Aaron Cushley, 2019
Edited by Sabrina Mahfouz

A CIP catalogue record for this book is available from the British Library.

ISBN 978 1 444 95124 0

Typeset in Adobe Caslon Pro by Avon DataSet Ltd,
Bidford-on-Avon, Warwickshire

Printed and bound in Great Britain by Clays Ltd, Elcograf S.p.A.

The paper and board used in this book are from wood from responsible sources.

Hodder Children's Books
An imprint of Hachette Children's Group
Part of Hodder & Stoughton
Carmelite House
50 Victoria Embankment
London EC4Y 0DZ

An Hachette UK Company
www.hachette.co.uk

www.hachettechildrens.co.uk

For all the little
planets in my life – Tabari,
Georgie, Caydee, Aaliyah, Sami,
Audrey, Carmen, Lou-Lou, Khari, Kioni,
Milo, Marley, Romy, Cleo, Leon,
Dan, Bill, Freija, Marcel, Sloan,
Arianna & Eisa.

Contents

Introduction   1

SUN SHINES

Aximu's Awakening   PAMELA C. MORDECAI   5

Chorus   DAVID RUDD-MITCHELL   7

New Every Morning   SUSAN COOLIDGE   8

From The Rubaiyat   OMAR KHAYYAM   10

From A Light Exists in Spring   EMILY DICKINSON   11

Weather Proverb   ANONYMOUS   12

Weather Proverb   ANONYMOUS   13

Sun and Flowers   MADISON JULIUS CAWEIN   14

The Sun   JOHN DRINKWATER   16

The Rooks   JANE EUPHEMIA BROWNE   17

Envoi   KATE SEYMOUR MACLEAN   18

From Strange Meetings   HAROLD MONRO   20

From How Clear, How Lovely Bright   A. E. HOUSMAN   21

Everything Is Going to Be All Right   DEREK MAHON   22

High Flight   JOHN GILLESPIE MAGEE   23

From The Sun Rising   JOHN DONNE   24

Composed Upon Westminster Bridge,
September 3, 1802   WILLIAM WORDSWORTH   25

The People Could Fly   GRACE NICHOLS   26

Picture a Vacuum   KATE TEMPEST   28

A Hymn to the Evening   PHILLIS WHEATLEY   30

Leisure   WILLIAM HENRY DAVIES   31

Everyone Sang   SIEGFRIED SASSOON   32

Eternity   WILLIAM BLAKE   33

Robin Redbreast   WILLIAM ALLINGHAM   34

Count That Day Lost   GEORGE ELIOT   36

A Little Song of Life   LIZETTE WOODWORTH REESE   37

This Ray   TRISKA HAMID   38

WIND BLOWS

Legend of the First Wind   JOELLE TAYLOR   43

Emily Hurricane   ALAN SMITH   46

White Sheep   ANONYMOUS   49

I Wandered Lonely as a Cloud   WILLIAM WORDSWORTH   50

Two Old Crows   VACHEL LINDSAY   52

Words   EDWARD THOMAS   54

Who Has Seen the Wind?   CHRISTINA ROSSETTI   57

The Thrush   FAY INCHFAWN   58

Prophecy   ELINOR WYLIE   59

The Roaring Frost   ALICE MEYNELL   60

Silent Messenger   LISA LUXX   61

Wallcracks   MAYSUN BINT BAHDAL   64

Answer to a Child's Question   SAMUEL TAYLOR COLERIDGE   65

The South Wind   ANONYMOUS   66

Thunder   ELIZABETH BISHOP   67

An Autumn Greeting   GEORGE COOPER   68

Weather Proverb   ANONYMOUS   70

A Lark   LAURENCE ALMA-TADEMA   71

The Storm   SARA COLERIDGE   72

The Wind   ROBERT LOUIS STEVENSON   73

The Eagle   ALFRED, LORD TENNYSON   74

How Can One Sell the Air?   CHIEF SEATTLE   75

Dis Breeze   VALERIE BLOOM   77

The Wind Shifts   WALLACE STEVENS   78

Tin Roof   NII AYIKWEI PARKES   79

Address to a Child During a Boisterous Winter
   Evening   DOROTHY WORDSWORTH   80

Once I Saw a Little Bird   ANONYMOUS   83

From Touch Him If You Dare   JULIANA HORATIA EWING   84

Someone Is Saved by Listening to the Nightingale
   GIOVANNI QUESSEP   85

Baby Seeds   ANONYMOUS   86

Summer Wind   WILLIAM CULLEN BRYANT   87

From A Make-Believe   GEORGE MACDONALD   89

From Great, Wide, Beautiful, Wonderful World
   WILLIAM BRIGHTY RANDS   90

You'll Never Walk Alone   OSCAR HAMMERSTEIN II   91

Birdland   ANONYMOUS   92

WATER FLOWS

With One Breath (Just One Breath!)   SIMON MOLE   97

Ariel's Song   WILLIAM SHAKESPEARE   100

Community Rain Song
   OODGEROO NOONUCCAL (KATH WALKER)   101

Rain on Dry Ground   CHRISTOPHER FRY   108

Waterfall Haiku   MATSUO BASHŌ   110

A Green Land Full of Rivers   SABRINA MAHFOUZ   111

Mail Drop   PAUL CAMERON BROWN   113

Until I Saw the Sea   LILIAN MOORE   115

A View of the Han River   WANG WEI   116

The Poet and the Brook   Juliana Horatia Ewing   117

Song of the Rain   Khalil Gibran   118

The Woodpecker   Elizabeth Madox Roberts   121

A Sea-Song   Sophie M. Hensley   122

Little Fish   D. H. Lawrence   124

Big Swimming   Edwin Ford Piper   125

Rainfall   Emily Pauline Johnson   126

Weather Proverb   Anonymous   127

From Wet Weather Talk   James Whitcomb Riley   128

The Crocodile   Lewis Carroll   129

Beachcomber   George Mackay Brown   130

The Deserted House   Mary Coleridge   132

Wynken, Blynken, and Nod   Eugene Field   133

Dancing   Yang Kuei-Fei   136

The Maldive Shark   Herman Melville   137

The Tide Rises, the Tide Falls
   Henry Wadsworth Longfellow   138

Duck's Ditty   Kenneth Grahame   139

A Beach on a Foggy Day   Jade Anouka   141

From The Scallop Shell   Dora Sigerson Shorter   143

Little Raindrops   Jane Euphemia Browne   144

Tsunami   Joydeb and Moyna Chitrakar   146

The Sea   Barry Cornwall   150

Laguna   Pratyusha   152

The Jumblies   Edward Lear   153

Ghazal with Rain and Birds   Shazea Quraishi   158

Sea Fever   John Masefield   159

Dover Beach   Matthew Arnold   160

Puddle   Kate Tempest   162

EARTH SPINS

The Spinning Earth   Aileen Fisher   169

Mother   oakley flanagan   170

The Worm   Ralph Bergengren   174

Counting-Out Rhyme   Edna St. Vincent Millay   175

From Childe Harold's Pilgrimage   Lord Byron   176

Enjoy the Earth   Traditional Yoruba   177

Pleasant Sounds   John Clare   178

Epigram for the Bald   Anonymous   179

Song   Paul Laurence Dunbar   180

Laverton Incident   Jack Davis   182

Autumn Evening   Matsuo Bashō   183

At Night I Talk to the Giant's Finger
   Stephen Lightbown   184

The Shadow of a Tree   West African Proverb   187

Once Upon a Time   Mary E. Wilkins Freeman   188

Anything!   Hollie McNish   189

Readjustment   Susan Coolidge   192

The Way Through the Woods   Rudyard Kipling   193

From Ode Number 7 from Book 4   Horace   195

Wood Between the Worlds   Iona Lee   196

Climbing   Amy Lowell   199

The Oak   Alfred, Lord Tennyson   200

Love is This Swamp   Deanna Rodger   201

The Statue   Ella Wheeler Wilcox   203

The Bashful Earthquake   Oliver Herford   205

Solitude   Archibald Lampman   206

Overheard on a Saltmarsh   Harold Monro   207

Peace and Pancakes   ADRIAN MITCHELL   208

Interim   LOLA RIDGE   212

Upon the Mountain's Distant Head
    WILLIAM CULLEN BRYANT   213

My Voice   PARTAW NADERI   214

My Heart's in the Highlands   ROBERT BURNS   215

I Sing of Change   NIYI OSUNDARE   216

I Am / I Say (children's choral song)   SABRINA MAHFOUZ   218

Earth Song   A. F. HARROLD   222

The Months   SARA COLERIDGE   224

A Song of a Navajo Weaver   BERTRAND N. O. WALKER   226

FIRE LEAPS

Bright Spark   MICHAELA MORGAN   231

Rainforest   JUDITH WRIGHT   232

Fire and Ice   ROBERT FROST   233

Fire in the Window   MARY MAPES DODGE   234

The Falling Star   SARA TEASDALE   235

From Life   EMILY DICKINSON   236

We the Fire Crowned Flares   HAFSAH ANEELA BASHIR   237

Paper   MONA ARSHI   239

The Tyger   WILLIAM BLAKE   242

Fire   DOROTHEA MACKELLAR   244

My Light with Yours   EDGAR LEE MASTERS   245

Thunder   ANNA AKHMATOVA   246

An Olive Fire   ROBERT WILLIAM SERVICE   247

All in June   WILLIAM HENRY DAVIES   249

First Fig   EDNA ST. VINCENT MILLAY   250

The Lights at Carney's Point
  ALICE MOORE DUNBAR-NELSON   251

From Home   MARIETTA HOLLEY   253

The Fire of Drift-Wood
  HENRY WADSWORTH LONGFELLOW   254

Weather Proverb   ANONYMOUS   257

Midsummer   WILLIAM CULLEN BRYANT   258

From The Aurora Australis   MARY HANNAY FOOTT   259

Flame Life   MAHD AL-AADIYYA   260

Across the Border   SOPHIE JEWETT   261

Flint   CHRISTINA ROSSETTI   262

Autumn Fires   ROBERT LOUIS STEVENSON   263

From The Firemen's Ball   VACHEL LINDSAY   264

LIFE GROWS

Stream of Life   RABINDRANATH TAGORE   275

Flowering Tree Haiku   MATSUO BASHŌ   276

From The Last Rose of Summer   THOMAS MOORE   277

The Snail's Monologue   CHRISTIAN MORGENSTERN   278

If I Were a Rose   SABRINA MAHFOUZ   279

A Toadstool Comes Up in a Night
  CHRISTINA ROSSETTI   280

The Bluebell   ANNE BRONTË   281

We Have a Little Garden   BEATRIX POTTER   284

Greek Proverb   ANONYMOUS   285

Tall Nettles   EDWARD THOMAS   286

Triolet   G. K. CHESTERTON   287

O Dandelion   ANONYMOUS   288

Twinshoots   Safiyya bint Khalid al-Bahiliyya   289

The Blackbird   Humbert Wolfe   290

Nature Poem   Talia Randall   291

I Went to the Animal Fair   Anonymous   293

How Pigeons Growl   Dean Atta   294

Winnebago Proverb   Traditional Native American   295

To a Squirrel at Kyle-Na-No   W. B. Yeats   296

The Microbe   Hilaire Belloc   297

With Birds You're Never Lonely   Raymond Antrobus   298

From Lines to a Shamrock – A Song of Exile
     Nora Pembroke   301

A Scherzo (A Shy Person's Wishes)   Dora Greenwell   302

How to Cut a Pomegranate   Imtiaz Dharker   304

I Dunno   Anonymous   306

From Antidote   Luka Lesson   307

Sonnet 15   William Shakespeare   308

A Soft White Feather Lying on the Grass
     Moniza Alvi   309

Rose and the Lily   Anonymous   310

Don't Cry, Caterpillar   Grace Nichols   311

A Guinea Pig   Anonymous   312

Sunflower   Marjorie Lotfi Gill   313

The Seedling   Paul Laurence Dunbar   314

Hurt No Living Thing   Christina Rossetti   316

The Little Green Man Addresses a Leaf   John Agard   317

Shuffle Monster   Dean Atta   318

ICE CHILLS

De   Valerie Bloom   323

From The Farewell Glacier   Nick Drake   325

From Snow-Bound   John Greenleaf Whittier   327

From Love's Labour's Lost   William Shakespeare   328

Wild Peaches   Elinor Wylie   329

White Fields   James Stephens   332

Weather Proverb   Anonymous   333

A Couplet   Itimad ar-Rumaikiyya   334

From London Snow   Robert Bridges   335

Dust of Snow   Robert Frost   336

February Twilight   Sara Teasdale   337

A Snow Man   Anonymous   338

Christmas Roses   Lizzie Lawson   339

Snowflakes   Leroy F. Jackson   340

Snow in the Suburbs   Thomas Hardy   341

Describing Snow in the Aftermath   Vanessa Kisuule   342

In the Garden   Anonymous   343

On the Hard Crest   Anna Akhmatova   344

Up in the Morning Early   Robert Burns   345

From With Solid Drops   Ibn Khafajah   346

Stopping by Woods on a Snowy Evening
    Robert Frost   347

From Snow   Eliza Cook   348

The Last Snow Leopard   Sabrina Mahfouz   349

Jack Frost   Celia Thaxter   351

Snow Pie Time   Salena Godden   352

The Skaters   JOHN GOULD FLETCHER   355

The Quiet Snow   RAYMOND KNISTER   356

Something Told the Wild Geese   RACHEL FIELD   357

Winter-Lull   D. H. LAWRENCE   358

A Windflower   LIZETTE WOODWORTH REESE   359

The Elephant is Walking on the River Thames
   IMTIAZ DHARKER   360

Snow Fox   LIZ BROWNLEE   362

From Frost at Midnight   SAMUEL TAYLOR COLERIDGE   364

The Thaw   HENRY DAVID THOREAU   365

Snow   EDWARD THOMAS   366

MOON RISES

The Moon Haiku   NIKYU   371

Dancing Disk in the Sky   HIBAQ OSMAN   372

Scottish Proverb   ANONYMOUS   374

Five Little Owls   ANONYMOUS   375

From Drifting Flowers of the Sea
   SADAKICHI HARTMANN   376

From Summer in London   HELEN LEAH REED   377

Seal Lullaby   RUDYARD KIPLING   378

Night   WILLIAM BLAKE   379

November Night   ADELAIDE CRAPSEY   382

From A Midsummer Night's Dream
   WILLIAM SHAKESPEARE   383

Weather Proverb   ANONYMOUS   384

Weather Proverb   ANONYMOUS   385

Spellbound   EMILY BRONTË   386

Beehive   JEAN TOOMER   387

What If the Moon Is a Refugee? SALENA GODDEN 388

Bedtime THOMAS HOOD 389

The Fog F. R. McCREARY 391

If You Were an Owl MARY MAPES DODGE 392

The Wind and the Moon GEORGE MACDONALD 393

Birch Trees JOHN RICHARD MORELAND 397

I Had a Boat MARY COLERIDGE 398

From The Starlight Night GERARD MANLEY HOPKINS 399

The Crescent Moon AMY LOWELL 400

The Algonquin Calendar of Changing Moons
CHERYL MOSKOWITZ 402

Summer Stars CARL SANDBURG 404

From The Bat JAMES WHITCOMB RILEY 405

Night Comes BEATRICE SCHENK DE REGNIERS 406

The Moon ROBERT LOUIS STEVENSON 407

From On the Road to the Sea CHARLOTTE MEW 408

Cushlamochree LUCY COATS 409

The Mother Moon LOUISA MAY ALCOTT 410

Morning Song SARA TEASDALE 412

My Brilliant Image HAFEZ 413

Index of first lines 415

Index of poets 423

Acknowledgements 427

Introduction

Poetry to take you all around the world? It really is possible. But can it take you time travelling? Yep, that too. Here are wonderful words from across the globe, under the waves, above the clouds, beneath the mud, but also from across the centuries – from a time before books were published all the way to this very year, words composed especially for this collection – for you.

Our planet is of course not just green and blue. It is yellow and red and brown and grey – there is actually a lot of grey! – and pink and black and orange and white and I have loved living amongst such colourful, constantly changing landscapes whilst compiling this epic book of poems.

I hope you also love living within these pages, wherever else you may be on our precious planet.

Sabrina Mahfouz, 2019

SUN SHINES

Tickling my eyes as usual

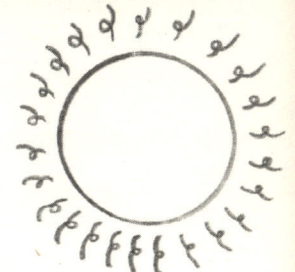

Aximu's Awakening

PAMELA C. MORDECAI

This morning the sun
tickled my eyes
as usual

and I slid from
my hammock
and looked at the skies
as usual

I yawned and I stretched
I felt like a splash
in the cold morning water
so I made a dash
towards the path
to the sea
before Ama could call me
and give me work.

As I burst through the bush
at the top of the hill

I froze and I shivered
my heart stood still.

Great canoes with houses
and clouds of cloth wings
hung on poles, full of wind,
strange, frightening things
on the sea!

'Great Iocuhuuague Maorocon'
I whispered and knew
those terrible canoes
were coming for me.

Chorus

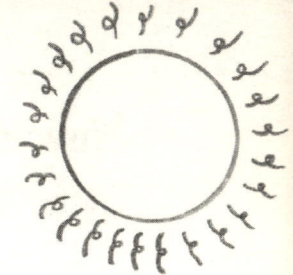

DAVID RUDD-MITCHELL

Soon,

The City's silence
will be broken.
And a day born.

When a blackbird sings,
From a high perch;
And announces dawn.

New Every Morning

SUSAN COOLIDGE

Every morn is the world made new.
You who are weary of sorrow and sinning,
Here is a beautiful hope for you,—
A hope for me and a hope for you.

All the past things are past and over;
The tasks are done and the tears are shed.
Yesterday's errors let yesterday cover;
Yesterday's wounds, which smarted and bled,
Are healed with the healing which night has shed.

Yesterday now is a part of forever,
Bound up in a sheaf, which God holds tight,
With glad days, and sad days, and bad days, which never
Shall visit us more with their bloom and their blight,
Their fulness of sunshine or sorrowful night.

Let them go, since we cannot re-live them,
Cannot undo and cannot atone;
God in his mercy receive, forgive them!

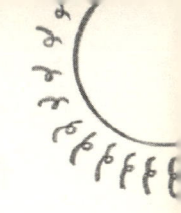

Only the new days are our own;
To-day is ours, and to-day alone.

Here are the skies all burnished brightly,
Here is the spent earth all re-born,
Here are the tired limbs springing lightly
To face the sun and to share with the morn
In the chrism of dew and the cool of dawn.

Every day is a fresh beginning;
Listen, my soul, to the glad refrain,
And, spite of old sorrow and older sinning,
And puzzles forecasted and possible pain,
Take heart with the day, and begin again.

From The Rubaiyat

OMAR KHAYYAM

Translated from the Persian by Edward Fitzgerald

Awake! for Morning in the Bowl of Night
Has flung the Stone that puts the Stars to Flight:
And Lo! the Hunter of the East has caught
The Sultan's Turret in a Noose of Light.

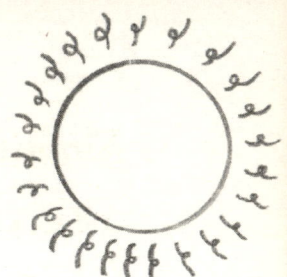

From A Light Exists in Spring

EMILY DICKINSON

A Light exists in Spring
Not present on the Year
At any other period —
When March is scarcely here

A Colour stands abroad
On Solitary Fields
That Science cannot overtake
But Human Nature feels.

It waits upon the Lawn,
It shows the furthest Tree
Upon the furthest Slope you know
It almost speaks to you.

Weather Proverb

ANONYMOUS

If woolly fleeces deck the heavenly way
Be sure no rain will mar a summer's day.

Weather Proverb

ANONYMOUS

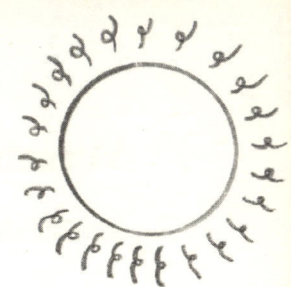

Sun sets Friday, clear as bell
Rain on Monday, sure as hell.

Sun and Flowers

MADISON JULIUS CAWEIN

The spring is coming! hear it blow!
The rain and wind have cleared the snow;
And I am going to play my fill
With sunlight on the windy hill.

And I am going to laugh and run,
And be the comrade of the sun;
And, like the wildflowers, wink my eyes
At him and at the springtime skies.

And I am going to leap and shout
And toss my hair and arms about,
And fill my soul with sunshine as
The blossoms do and waving grass.

And I am going to dance and sing
And match the swallow on the wing,
And put my arms about each tree,
And kiss it as the sun does me.

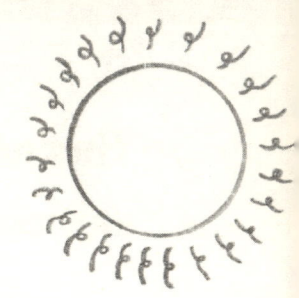

And I am going to lie face down
Upon the hillside, far from town,
And hug it as the sunlight does,
And watch the pussy-willows fuzz.

I wish I was as big and bright
As is the sunlight: then I might
Hold all the hillside in my joy
But I am just a little boy.

And I am only sweet and small
As are the wildflowers, that is all,
So mother says; and thus you see
The sun can get ahead of me.

Blow wind and rain! and sweep away
The snow and sleet of yesterday!
And bring the sunlight and the flowers
And all the laughing springtime hours.

The Sun

JOHN DRINKWATER

I told the Sun that I was glad,
I'm sure I don't know why;
Somehow the pleasant way he had
Of shining in the sky,
Just put a notion in my head
That wouldn't it be fun
If, walking on the hill, I said
"I'm happy" to the Sun.

The Rooks

JANE EUPHEMIA BROWNE

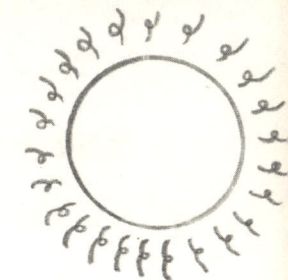

The rooks are building on the trees;
They build there every spring:
"Caw, caw," is all they say,
For none of them can sing.

They're up before the break of day,
And up till late at night;
For they must labour busily
As long as it is light.

And many a crooked stick they bring,
And many a slender twig,
And many a tuft of moss, until
Their nests are round and big.

"Caw, caw!" Oh, what a noise
They make in rainy weather!
Good children always speak by turns,
But rooks all talk together.

Envoi

KATE SEYMOUR MACLEAN

A little bird woke singing in the night,
    Dreaming of coming day,
And piped, for very fulness of delight,
    His little roundelay.

Dreaming he heard the wood-lark's carol loud,
    Down calling to his mate,
Like silver rain out of a golden cloud,
    At morning's radiant gate.

And all for joy of his embowering woods,
    And dewy leaves he sung,—
The summer sunshine, and the summer floods
    By forest flowers o'erhung.

Thou shalt not hear those wild and sylvan notes
    When morn's full chorus pours
Rejoicing from a thousand feathered throats,
    And the lark sings and soars,

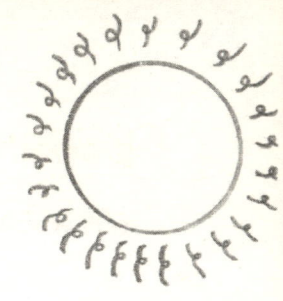

Oh poet of our glorious land so fair,
  Whose foot is at the door;
Even so my song shall melt into the air,
  And die and be no more.

But thou shalt live, part of the nation's life;
  The world shall hear thy voice
Singing above the noise of war and strife,
  And therefore I rejoice!

From **Strange Meetings**

HAROLD MONRO

The stars must make an awful noise
In whirling round the sky;
Yet somehow I can't even hear
Their loudest song or sigh.

So it is wonderful to think
One blackbird can outsing
The voice of all the swarming stars
On any day in Spring.

From How Clear, How Lovely Bright

A. E. HOUSMAN

How clear, how lovely bright,
How beautiful to sight
Those beams of morning play;
How heaven laughs out with glee
Where, like a bird set free,
Up from the eastern sea
Soars the delightful day.

Everything Is Going to Be All Right

DEREK MAHON

How should I not be glad to contemplate
the clouds clearing beyond the dormer window
and a high tide reflected on the ceiling?
There will be dying, there will be dying,
but there is no need to go into that.
The poems flow from the hand unbidden
and the hidden source is the watchful heart.
The sun rises in spite of everything
and the far cities are beautiful and bright.
I lie here in a riot of sunlight
watching the day break and the clouds flying.
Everything is going to be all right.

High Flight

JOHN GILLESPIE MAGEE

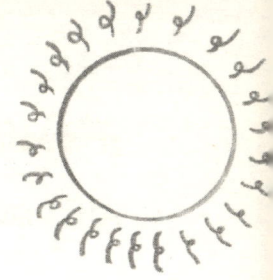

Oh! I have slipped the surly bonds of Earth
And danced the skies on laughter-silvered wings;
Sunward I've climbed, and joined the tumbling mirth
Of sun-split clouds, – and done a hundred things
You have not dreamed of – wheeled and soared and
   swung
High in the sunlit silence. Hov'ring there,
I've chased the shouting wind along, and flung
My eager craft through footless halls of air...

Up, up the long, delirious burning blue
I've topped the wind-swept heights with easy grace
Where never lark, or ever eagle flew –
And, while with silent, lifting mind I've trod
The high untrespassed sanctity of space,
Put out my hand, and touched the face of God.

From The Sun Rising

JOHN DONNE

Busy old fool, unruly sun,
   Why dost thou thus,
Through windows, and through curtains call on us?

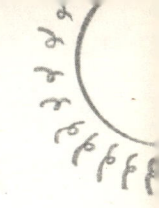

Composed Upon Westminster Bridge, September 3, 1802

WILLIAM WORDSWORTH

Earth has not anything to show more fair:
Dull would he be of soul who could pass by
A sight so touching in its majesty:
This City now doth, like a garment, wear
The beauty of the morning; silent, bare,
Ships, towers, domes, theatres, and temples lie
Open unto the fields, and to the sky;
All bright and glittering in the smokeless air.
Never did sun more beautifully steep
In his first splendour, valley, rock, or hill;
Ne'er saw I, never felt, a calm so deep!
The river glideth at his own sweet will:
Dear God! the very houses seem asleep;
And all that mighty heart is lying still!

The People Could Fly

GRACE NICHOLS

The people could fly –
See them rise up, a cloud of locusts
or more a host of scarecrows in suneye?
Wind flapping against their
sunworn dresses and tattered shirt-coats

This brethren who lived a life
of saltless endurance.
No slave-food – salt beef, saltfish,
to blight their blood or mock the freedom,
the heady helium gathering slowly in their veins.

How closely they guarded their levitational-mystery
How calmly they carried out their earthly duties
And now it's lift-off time –
See them making for the
green open hilltops
with nothing but their faith
and their corncobs?

Hear them singing; One bright morning
when my work is over I will fly away home…

The people could fly.
Look! Look, how they coming, Africa!
'Goodbye plantation goodbye.'

*This poem is based on an old African belief that if you declined to
eat salt, then your soul would grow light enough to fly.*

Picture a Vacuum

KATE TEMPEST

Picture a vacuum
An endless and unmoving blackness
Peace, or the absence at least, of terror
I see, and amongst all this space
That speck of light in the furthest corner
Gold as a pharaoh's coffin
Now follow that light with your tired eyes
It's been a long day, I know, but look
Watch as it flickers and it roars into fullness and fills the
  whole frame
Blazing a fire you can't bear the majesty of
Here is our Sun
And look
See how the planets are dangled around it
And held in that intricate dance
There is our Earth
Our Earth
Its blueness soothes the sharp burn in your eyes
Its contours remind you of love
That soft roundness
The comfort of ocean and land mass

Picture the world

Older than she ever thought that she'd get

She looks at herself as she spins

Arms loaded with the trophies of her most successful
child

The pylons and mines

The powerplants shimmer in her still, cool breath

Now, is that a smile that plays across her lips

Or is it a tremor of dread?

The sadness of mothers as they watch the fates of their
children unfold

A Hymn to the Evening

PHILLIS WHEATLEY

Soon as the sun forsook the eastern main
The pealing thunder shook the heav'nly plain;
Majestic grandeur! From the zephyr's wing,
Exhales the incense of the blooming spring.
Soft purl the streams, the birds renew their notes,
And through the air their mingled music floats.
Through all the heav'ns what beauteous dies are spread!
But the west glories in the deepest red:
So may our breasts with ev'ry virtue glow,
The living temples of our God below!
Fill'd with the praise of him who gives the light,
And draws the sable curtains of the night,
Let placid slumbers sooth each weary mind,
At morn to wake more heav'nly, more refin'd;
So shall the labours of the day begin
More pure, more guarded from the snares of sin.
Night's leaden sceptre seals my drowsy eyes,
Then cease, my song, till fair *Aurora* rise.

Leisure

WILLIAM HENRY DAVIES

What is this life if, full of care,
We have no time to stand and stare?—

No time to stand beneath the boughs,
And stare as long as sheep and cows:

No time to see, when woods we pass,
Where squirrels hide their nuts in grass:

No time to see, in broad daylight,
Streams full of stars, like skies at night:

No time to turn at Beauty's glance,
And watch her feet, how they can dance:

No time to wait till her mouth can
Enrich that smile her eyes began?

A poor life this if, full of care,
We have no time to stand and stare.

Everyone Sang

SIEGFRIED SASSOON

Everyone suddenly burst out singing;
And I was filled with such delight
As prisoned birds must find in freedom,
Winging wildly across the white
Orchards and dark-green fields; on – on – and out of
   sight.

Everyone's voice was suddenly lifted;
And beauty came like the setting sun:
My heart was shaken with tears; and horror
Drifted away… O, but Everyone
Was a bird; and the song was wordless; the singing will
   never be done.

Eternity

WILLIAM BLAKE

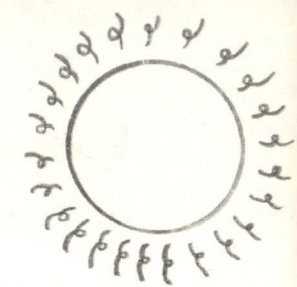

He who binds to himself a joy
Does the winged life destroy;
But he who kisses the joy as it flies
Lives in eternity's sun rise.

Robin Redbreast

WILLIAM ALLINGHAM

Goodbye, goodbye to Summer!
For Summer's nearly done;
The garden smiling faintly,
Cool breezes in the sun;
Our Thrushes now are silent,
Our Swallows flown away-
But Robin's here, in coat of brown,
With ruddy breast-knot gay.
Robin, Robin Redbreast,
O Robin dear!
Robin singing sweetly
In the falling of the year.

Bright yellow, red, and orange,
The leaves come down in hosts;
The trees are Indian Princes,
But soon they'll turn to Ghosts;
The leathery pears and apples
Hang russet on the bough,
It's Autumn, Autumn, Autumn late,
'Twill soon be winter now.

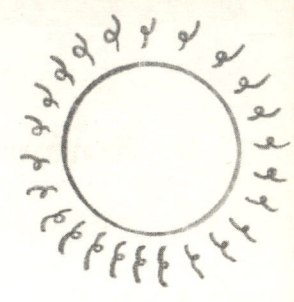

Robin, Robin Redbreast,
O Robin dear!
And what will this poor Robin do?
For pinching days are near.

The fireside for the Cricket,
The wheatsack for the Mouse,
When trembling night-winds whistle
And moan all round the house;
The frosty ways like iron,
The branches plumed with snow –
Alas! in Winter, dead, and dark,
Where can poor Robin go?
Robin, Robin Redbreast,
O Robin dear!
And a crumb of bread for Robin,
His little heart to cheer.

Count That Day Lost

GEORGE ELIOT (MARY ANN EVANS)

If you sit down at set of sun
And count the acts that you have done,
And, counting, find
One self-denying deed, one word
That eased the heart of him who heard,
One glance most kind
That fell like sunshine where it went—
Then you may count that day well spent.

But if, through all the livelong day,
You've cheered no heart, by yea or nay—
If, through it all
You've nothing done that you can trace
That brought the sunshine to one face—
No act most small
That helped some soul and nothing cost—
Then count that day as worse than lost.

A Little Song of Life

LIZETTE WOODWORTH REESE

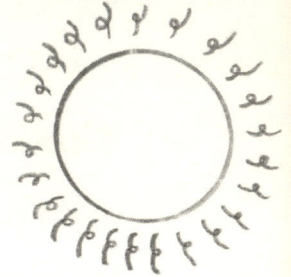

Glad that I live am I;
That the sky is blue;
Glad for the country lanes,
And the fall of dew.

After the sun the rain,
After the rain the sun;
This is the way of life,
Till the work be done.

All that we need to do,
Be we low or high,
Is to see that we grow
Nearer the sky.

This Ray

TRISKA HAMID

This ray of sun I claim
When warmth begins to wane.
On days when darkness lingers
In cold and ghastly winters,
I'll recall its intensity
That day it shined in me.

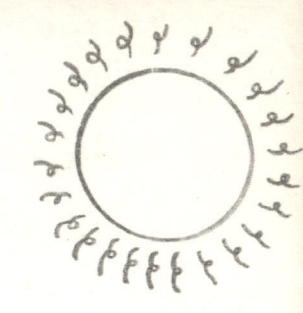

WIND BLOWS

BETWEEN WHAT WARNING SEAS
AND CONQUERING SKIES...

Legend of the First Wind

JOELLE TAYLOR

In the small time
when stones were water and trees walked the earth
the wind was a small child singing

She wrote her names on Saharan sand
Mistral, Sirocco, Khamseen, Bora, Brickfielder
prevailing Westerly to the breath of her melody

In her pockets she carried
Frangipani, cocoa, tea, the seven spices
sprinkling trade ballads across dry and tall

Her song made the ocean dance
rear on its hind legs, clapping wet hands
as it rode to shore on the horse-winds

Her compass winds were hymns
to wet foot and washing lines
below her children coloured the cities in

until she came to a wall
as thick as language
and could move no further forward.

The cities stopped and stared at the wall.
The air thickened and stood silent
listening to the song beyond the bricks.

Without wind they could not breathe
the earth stung their feet
and the heat was a stalking lion

Then a brown bird dropped from the sky
onto the hand of the small child singing, and whispered
let me carry you little daughter

Birds cannot see borders
so she carried the wind in her beak
and sang it across the land

To this day
birds carry the wind to the town and cities
high above check points and ports

In the small time
when stones were water and trees walked the earth
the wind was a small child singing

listen

Emily Hurricane

ALAN SMITH

Woke up this morning
to a breakfast sky,
fed the kitten marmalade,
had some sunshine in my tea
and then went out to greet the day,
met Miss Emily Hurricane.

She said
Wouldn't you like to swim in the sky,
sail with the trees as they go whizzing by,
dance with the rooftops as they go bubbling?
Wouldn't you like to swim in the sky?

She had silver hair
but it was kind of wild,

electricity for eyes
and a crackling laugh,
ranting and raving
like she was crazy.

She kept singing to me
Wouldn't you like to swim in the sky
sail with the trees as they go whizzing by,
dance with the rooftops as they go bubbling?
Wouldn't you like to swim in the sky?

I asked her,
'Why are you howling
outside my windows?'
She answered,
'Rounding up beaches to herd away
and deliver to a better place.'

And the beaches like white sheep but sad,
their beauty blemished with tar and debris,
were elated to run away with her
and find a safer home at the bottom of the sea.

As they left she whistled,
Wouldn't you like to swim in the sky,
sail with the trees as they go whizzing by,
dance with the rooftops as they go bubbling?
Wouldn't you like to swim in the sky?

I shouted in reply,
'Maybe I'd like to join the beaches
at the bottom of the sea.'
As she disappeared I heard her sing,
'If you ever make it to the bottom of the sea
you can join us as we dance, the beaches and me.'

White Sheep

ANONYMOUS

White sheep, white sheep,
On a blue hill,
When the wind stops
You all stand still.

When the wind blows,
You walk away slow.
White sheep, white sheep,
Where do you go?

I Wandered Lonely as a Cloud

WILLIAM WORDSWORTH

(last two lines by Mary Wordsworth)

I wandered lonely as a cloud
That floats on high o'er vales and hills,
When all at once I saw a crowd,
A host, of golden daffodils;
Beside the lake, beneath the trees,
Fluttering and dancing in the breeze.

Continuous as the stars that shine
And twinkle on the milky way,
They stretched in never-ending line
Along the margin of a bay:
Ten thousand saw I at a glance,
Tossing their heads in sprightly dance.

The waves beside them danced; but they
Out-did the sparkling waves in glee:
A poet could not but be gay,
In such a jocund company:
I gazed – and gazed – but little thought
What wealth the show to me had brought:

For oft, when on my couch I lie
In vacant or in pensive mood,
They flash upon that inward eye
Which is the bliss of solitude;
And then my heart with pleasure fills,
And dances with the daffodils.

Two Old Crows

VACHEL LINDSAY

Two old crows sat on a fence rail.
Two old crows sat on a fence rail,
Thinking of effect and cause,
Of weeds and flowers,
And nature's laws.
One of them muttered, one of them stuttered,
One of them stuttered, one of them muttered.
Each of them thought far more than he uttered.
One crow asked the other crow a riddle.
One crow asked the other crow a riddle:
The muttering crow
Asked the stuttering crow,
"Why does a bee have a sword to his fiddle?
Why does a bee have a sword to his fiddle?"
"Bee-cause," said the other crow,
"Bee-cause,
B B B B B B B B B B B B B B B B B-cause."

Just then a bee flew close to their rail:—
"Buzzzzzzzzzzzzzzzzzzzz zzzzzzzzz zzzzzzzzzzzzzzz
ZZZZZZZZ."

And those two black crows

Turned pale,

And away those crows did sail.

Why?

B B B B B B B B B B B B B B B B-cause.

B B B B B B B B B B B B B B B B B-cause.

"Buzzzzzzzzzzzzzzzzzz zzzzzzzzz zzzzzzzzzzzzzzzz
ZZZZZZZZ."

Words

EDWARD THOMAS

Out of us all
That make rhymes
Will you choose
Sometimes –
As the winds use
A crack in a wall
Or a drain,
Their joy or their pain
To whistle through –
Choose me,
You English words?

I know you:
You are light as dreams,
Tough as oak,
Precious as gold,
As poppies and corn,
Or an old cloak:
Sweet as our birds
To the ear,
As the burnet rose

In the heat
Of Midsummer:
Strange as the races
Of dead and unborn:
Strange and sweet
Equally,
And familiar,
To the eye,
As the dearest faces
That a man knows,
And as lost homes are:
But though older far
Than oldest yew, –
As our hills are, old, –
Worn new
Again and again:
Young as our streams
After rain:
And as dear
As the earth which you prove
That we love.

Make me content
With some sweetness

From Wales
Whose nightingales
Have no wings, –
From Wiltshire and Kent
And Herefordshire, –
And the villages there, –
From the names, and the things
No less.
Let me sometimes dance
With you,
Or climb
Or stand perchance
In ecstasy,
Fixed and free
In a rhyme,
As poets do.

Who Has Seen the Wind?

CHRISTINA ROSSETTI

Who has seen the wind?
Neither I nor you:
But when the leaves hang trembling,
The wind is passing through.

Who has seen the wind?
Neither you nor I:
But when the trees bow down their heads,
The wind is passing by.

The Thrush

FAY INCHFAWN

Across the land came a magic word
When the earth was bare and lonely,
And I sit and sing of the joyous spring,
For 'twas I who heard, I only!
Then dreams came by, of the gladsome days,
Of many a wayside posy;
For a crocus peeps where the wild rose sleeps,
And the willow wands are rosy!

Oh! the time to be! When the paths are green,
When the primrose-gold is lying
'Neath the hazel spray, where the catkins sway,
And the dear south wind comes sighing.

My mate and I, we shall build a nest,
So snug and warm and cosy,
When the kingcups gleam on the meadow stream,
Where the willow wands are rosy!

Prophecy

ELINOR WYLIE

I shall die hidden in a hut
In the middle of an alder wood,
With the back door blind and bolted shut,
And the front door locked for good.

I shall lie folded like a saint,
Lapped in a scented linen sheet,
On a bedstead striped with bright-blue paint,
Narrow and cold and neat.

The midnight will be glassy black
Behind the panes, with wind about
To set his mouth against a crack
And blow the candle out.

The Roaring Frost

ALICE MEYNELL

A flock of winds came winging from the North,
   Strong birds with fighting pinions driving forth
     With a resounding call!

Where will they close their wings and cease their cries—
   Between what warming seas and conquering skies—
     And fold, and fall?

Silent Messenger

LISA LUXX

You say, "Welcome in, Air
May my body be a resting house
I tidied up the place
Please use my lungs as a lounge."

"Thank you," air replies
In no uncertain sigh
But never goes on to say:

You know, I've had a long day
I carried a flock of birds
To find food and nesting.
In return, I brought their song
And passed it on to the dawn
Who played it during sunrise
To brighten everybody's morning.

And how proud I am to tell you
I've planted future trees!
Delivering to greenest fields
Our forest's pregnant seeds.

Then under the heat of sun
I threw down a steady net
Gathered drops of water
Which I fed to the clouds.
What was left I offered
To the mountain's
Icy mouths.

You see air is the silent martyr
A messenger of sound and seed
Invisible to the naked eye
It performs the hand of god so elegantly.

You could be forgiven if you never realised
That everything from soil to skies
Is kept alive by the winds.
Yet air never speaks a peep of this
When on breath, it comes in.
Humble as the air is
We must imagine what it's speaking:

Some time ago,
I opened up my pockets
To give smoke a place to hide.
Since then I've carried it
Around the world twice.

You see I'm like a prayer
Travelling everywhere
Before trusting you
With another gust of life.

Consider the mistake you make
When you barely open your lungs,
As if air isn't welcome to stay.
Inhale these resting angels
As they file in home for tea.

In return Air will bring your body
A new burst of energy.
As the jaw lets go of all it holds
Your inner child laughs and play
Wounds close their lips
And the intestines relax
For the first time in days.

Say your praise.
Then let it go.
Offering a farewell song
To the silent messenger
Who heads back out to the world it holds.

Wallcracks

MAYSUN BINT BAHDAL

Translated from the Arabic by Abdullah Al-Udhari

I'd rather listen to the winds voicing
through wallcracks than to the sound of tambourines.

Answer to a Child's Question

SAMUEL TAYLOR COLERIDGE

Do you ask what the birds say? The sparrow, the dove,
The linnet and thrush say, "I love and I love!"
In the winter they're silent – the wind is so strong;
What it says, I don't know, but it sings a loud song.
But green leaves, and blossoms, and sunny warm
   weather,
And singing, and loving – all come back together.
But the Lark is so brimful of gladness and love,
The green fields below him, the blue sky above,
That he sings, and he sings; and for ever sings he—
"I love my Love, and my Love loves me!

The South Wind

ANONYMOUS

The south wind brings wet weather;
The north wind wet and cold together;
The west wind always brings us rain;
The east wind blows it back again.

Thunder

ELIZABETH BISHOP

And suddenly the giants tired of play. –
With huge, rough hands they flung the gods' gold balls
And silver harps and mirrors at the walls
Of Heaven, and trod, ashamed, where lay
The loveliness of flowers. Frightened Day
On white feet ran from out the temple halls,
The blundering dark was filled with great war-calls,
And Beauty, shamed, slunk silently away.

Be quiet, little wind among the leaves
That turn pale faces to the coming storm.
Be quiet, little foxes in your lairs,
And birds and mice be still – a giant grieves
For his forgotten might. Hark now the warm
And heavy stumbling down the leaden stairs!

An Autumn Greeting

GEORGE COOPER

"Come, little leaves," said the wind one day,
"Come o'er the meadows with me and play;
Put on your dresses of red and gold,
For summer is gone and the days grow cold."

Soon as the leaves heard the wind's loud call,
Down they came fluttering, one and all;
Over the brown fields they danced and flew,
Singing the glad little songs they knew.

"Cricket, good-by, we've been friends so long,
Little brook, sing us your farewell song;
Say you are sorry to see us go;
Ah, you will miss us, right well we know.

"Dear little lambs in your fleecy fold,
Mother will keep you from harm and cold;
Fondly we watched you in vale and glade,
Say, will you dream of our loving shade?"

Dancing and whirling, the little leaves went,
Winter had called them, and they were content;
Soon, fast asleep in their earthy beds,
The snow laid a coverlid over their heads.

Weather Proverb

ANONYMOUS

March winds bring April showers
April showers bring May flowers.

A Lark

LAURENCE ALMA-TADEMA

Lark-bird, lark-bird soaring high,
Are you never weary?
When you reach the empty sky,
Are the clouds not dreary?
Don't you sometimes long to be
A silent gold-fish in the sea?

Gold-fish, gold-fish diving deep,
Are you never sad, say?
When you feel the cold waves creep
Are you really glad, say?
Don't you sometimes long to sing
And be a lark-bird on the wing?

The Storm

SARA COLERIDGE

See lightening is flashing,
The forest is crashing,
The rain will come dashing,
A flood will be rising anon;
The heavens are scowling,
The thunder is growling,
The loud winds are howling,
The storm has come suddenly on!
But now the sky clears,
The bright sun appears,
Now nobody fears,
But soon every cloud will be gone.

The Wind

ROBERT LOUIS STEVENSON

I saw you toss the kites on high
And blow the birds about the sky;
And all around I heard you pass,
Like ladies' skirts across the grass—
    O wind, a-blowing all day long,
    O wind, that sings so loud a song!

I saw the different things you did,
But always you yourself you hid.
I felt you push, I heard you call,
I could not see yourself at all—
    O wind, a-blowing all day long,
    O wind, that sings so loud a song!

O you that are so strong and cold,
O blower, are you young or old?
Are you a beast of field and tree,
Or just a stronger child than me?
    O wind, a-blowing all day long,
    O wind, that sings so loud a song!

The Eagle

ALFRED, LORD TENNYSON

He clasps the crag with crooked hands;
Close to the sun in lonely lands,
Ring'd with the azure world, he stands.

The wrinkled sea beneath him crawls;
He watches from his mountain walls,
And like a thunderbolt he falls.

How Can One Sell the Air?

CHIEF SEATTLE

How can one sell the air
or buy the warmth of the earth?
It is difficult for us to imagine.
If we don't own the sweet air
or the bubbling water,
how can you buy it from us?
Each hillside of pines shining in the sun,
each sandy beach and rocky river bank,
every steep valley with bees humming
or mists hanging in dark woods,
has been made sacred by some event
in the memory of our people.

We are part of the earth
and the earth is part of us.
The fragrant flowers are our sisters;
the reindeer, the horse,
the great eagles, are our brothers.
The foamy crests of waves in the river,
the sap of meadow flowers,
the pony's sweat and the man's sweat

are one and the same thing.
So when the Great Chief in Washington
sends word he wants to buy all these things,
we find it hard to understand.

This is part of a speech made in 1854 by a Native American tribal chief in preparation for the Indian Land Treaties.

Dis Breeze

VALERIE BLOOM

Dis breeze is an air conditioner,
Dis breeze better than any fan,
Dis breeze blow soft an' warm
Dry me face an' foot an' han.

Dis breeze don't have no manners,
Dis breeze is much too bold,
Look how dis breeze lift up me skirt
And show me knickers to the world!

The Wind Shifts

WALLACE STEVENS

This is how the wind shifts:
Like the thoughts of an old human,
Who still thinks eagerly
And despairingly.
The wind shifts like this:
Like a human without illusions,
Who still feels irrational things within her.
The wind shifts like this:
Like humans approaching proudly,
Like humans approaching angrily.
This is how the wind shifts:
Like a human, heavy and heavy,
Who does not care.

Tin Roof

NII AYIKWEI PARKES

Wild harmattan winds whip you
but still you stay;
they spit dust all over your gleam
and twist your sharp cutting edges.
The rains come zinging mud
with their own tapping music
yet you remain
– my pride –
my very own tin roof.

Address to a Child During a Boisterous Winter Evening

DOROTHY WORDSWORTH

What way does the wind come? What way does he go?
He rides over the water, and over the snow,
Through wood, and through vale; and o'er rocky height,
Which the goat cannot climb, takes his sounding flight;
He tosses about in every bare tree,
As, if you look up, you plainly may see;
But how he will come, and whither he goes,
There's never a scholar in England knows.

He will suddenly stop in a cunning nook,
And ring a sharp 'larum; but, if you should look,
There's nothing to see but a cushion of snow,
Round as a pillow, and whiter than milk,
And softer than if it were covered with silk.
Sometimes he'll hide in the cave of a rock,
Then whistle as shrill as the buzzard cock;
– Yet seek him, and what shall you find in the place?
Nothing but silence and empty space;
Save, in a corner, a heap of dry leaves,
That he's left, for a bed, to beggars or thieves!

As soon as 'tis daylight tomorrow, with me
You shall go to the orchard, and then you will see
That he has been there, and made a great rout,
And cracked the branches, and strewn them about;
Heaven grant that he spare but that one upright twig
That looked up at the sky so proud and big
All last summer, as well you know,
Studded with apples, a beautiful show!

Hark! over the roof he makes a pause,
And growls as if he would fix his claws
Right in the slates, and with a huge rattle
Drive them down, like men in a battle:
– But let him range round; he does us no harm,
We build up the fire, we're snug and warm;
Untouched by his breath see the candle shines bright,
And burns with a clear and steady light.

Books have we to read, but that half-stifled knell,
Alas! 'tis the sound of the eight o'clock bell.
– Come, now we'll to bed! and when we are there
He may work his own will, and what shall we care?
He may knock at the door – we'll not let him in;
May drive at the windows – we'll laugh at his din;

Let him seek his own home wherever it be;
Here's a *cozie* warm house for Edward and me.

Once I Saw a Little Bird

ANONYMOUS

Once I saw a little bird
going hop, hop, hop.
So I cried, 'Little bird,
will you stop, stop, stop?'
And was going to the window
to say, 'How do you do?'
When he shook his tail
and away he flew.

From Touch Him If You Dare

JULIANA HORATIA EWING

"At my time of life," said the Dandelion,
"I keep an eye on
The slightest sign of disturbance and riot,
For my one object is to keep quiet
The reason I take such very great care,"
The old Dandy went on, "is because of my hair.
It was very thick once, and as yellow as gold;
But now I am old,
It is snowy-white,
And comes off with the slightest fright.
As to using a brush—
My good dog! I beseech you, don't rush,
Go quietly by me, if you please
You're as bad as a breeze.
I hope you'll attend to what we've said;
And — whatever you do — don't touch my head,
In this equinoctial, blustering weather
You might knock it off with a feather."

Someone Is Saved by Listening to the Nightingale

GIOVANNI QUESSEP

Translated from the Spanish by Felipe Quintama and Ranald Barnicot

Let's say that one evening
The nightingale sang
On this rock
For just the touch of it
Time does not hurt us
Not everything is yours oblivion
Something remains
Among the ruins I ponder
That he'll never be dust
Who saw its flight
Or heard its song

Baby Seeds

ANONYMOUS

In a milkweed cradle
Snug and warm,
Baby seeds are hiding
Safe from harm.
Open wide the cradle,
Hold it high!
Come Mr Wind,
Help them fly.

Summer Wind

WILLIAM CULLEN BRYANT

It is a sultry day; the sun has drunk
The dew that lay upon the morning grass;
There is no rustling in the lofty elm
That canopies my dwelling, and its shade
Scarce cools me. All is silent, save the faint
And interrupted murmur of the bee,
Settling on the sick flowers, and then again
Instantly on the wing. The plants around
Feel the too potent fervours: the tall maize
Rolls up its long green leaves; the clover droops
Its tender foliage, and declines its blooms.
But far in the fierce sunshine tower the hills,
With all their growth of woods, silent and stern,
As if the scorching heat and dazzling light
Were but an element they loved. Bright clouds,
Motionless pillars of the brazen heaven—
Their bases on the mountains – their white tops
Shining in the far ether – fire the air
With a reflected radiance, and make turn
The gazer's eye away. For me, I lie
Languidly in the shade, where the thick turf,

Yet virgin from the kisses of the sun,
Retains some freshness, and I woo the wind
That still delays his coming. Why so slow,
Gentle and voluble spirit of the air?
Oh, come and breathe upon the fainting earth
Coolness and life! Is it that in his caves
He hears me? See, on yonder woody ridge,
The pine is bending his proud top, and now
Among the nearer groves, chestnut and oak
Are tossing their green boughs about. He comes;
Lo, where the grassy meadow runs in waves!
The deep distressful silence of the scene
Breaks up with mingling of unnumbered sounds
And universal motion. He is come,
Shaking a shower of blossoms from the shrubs,
And bearing on their fragrance; and he brings
Music of birds, and rustling of young boughs,
And sound of swaying branches, and the voice
Of distant waterfalls. All the green herbs
Are stirring in his breath; a thousand flowers,
By the road-side and the borders of the brook,
Nod gayly to each other; glossy leaves
Are twinkling in the sun, as if the dew
Were on them yet, and silver waters break
Into small waves and sparkle as he comes.

From **A Make-Believe**

GEORGE MACDONALD

I will think as thinks the rabbit…

…Let the wind chafe
In the trees overhead,
We are quite safe
In our dark, yellow bed!
Let the rain pour!
It never can bore
A hole in our roof –
It is waterproof!
So is the cloak
We always carry,
We furry folk,
In sandhole or quarry!

From Great, Wide, Beautiful, Wonderful World

WILLIAM BRIGHTY RANDS

Great, wide, beautiful, wonderful World,
With the wonderful water round you curled,
And the wonderful grass upon your breast,
World, you are beautifully dressed.

The wonderful air is over me:
And the wonderful wind is shaking the tree,
It walks on the water, and whirls the mills,
And talks to itself on top of the hills.

You'll Never Walk Alone

OSCAR HAMMERSTEIN II

When you walk through a storm
Hold your chin up high
And don't be afraid of the dark.
At the end of a storm
Is a golden sky
And the sweet, silver song of a lark.
Walk on, through the wind,
Walk on, through the rain,
Though your dreams be tossed and blown.
Walk on, walk on with hope in your heart,
And you'll never walk alone,
You'll never walk alone.

Birdland

ANONYMOUS

I can remember
The first time I flew.
The thrill of the take-off
The joy of the lift
The victory over gravity.
I so enjoyed
Cruising over clouds,
I so enjoyed
Looking out for angels,
How I enjoyed
Looking down
On the tiny people below
And wondering
If they were looking up at me
And wondering.

The birds were cool.
Flying is wonderful
And landing is exciting.
Yes I can remember
The first time I flew.

It was great.
I still fly
Every now and then
But now I use aeroplanes.

WATER FLOWS

AROUND A GREEN LAND FULL OF
RIVERS AND WARM TO THE
TOUCH RAIN...

With One Breath (Just One Breath!)

SIMON MOLE

dive deep beneath the waves of the Sulu Sea
down where the stretching fingers of the sun can't reach
where two feet   kick   kick   like
   fishes flippers
pushing closer to the ocean's floor,
the coral reef.

With One Breath (Just One Breath!)
the owner of these feet is on a search for supper
Sulbin's 20 metres under, wearing nothing but goggles
and tiny blue trunks.

In his lungs that breath gets condensed
you know squashed or squeezed
by the pressure of the water
which he pulls from his path like he was scooping ice
   cream
      in slooooooooooow mo
Sulbin takes giant strides   so slow across the sea-bed
his feet pressed against rough sand and crushed crab
   shells.

The breath is banging on the walls of Sulbin's chest to be
     let out!

Six little fish nip past in quick darts.
                    Two tiny sea spiders scurry under a rock.

Now imagine that your kitchen had the biggest fridge in
but when you open the door all the food runs off!
That's the feeling Sulbin's got.
When suddenly
                    he spots an almost plate shaped fish
         black with yellow stripes and
heading for some wavy green seaweed
                    GO!
Reaction time sharper than a shark's tooth
Sulbin's arms move, firing his harpoon straight
through the middle of the fish
Keeping it tight within his grip, he surges to the surface
blowing out a stream of bubbles
from that One Breath (Just One Breath!)
 a stream of bubbles which dance
the happy dance of the nearly home
          "Here we go!"

Sulbin shoots out from the water
shaking the wet hair on his head from side to side
still clutching his fish
he lifts it up towards the sky
where its wet skin sparkles in the sun
shining bright like a trophy
One Breath (Just One Breath!)

*The Bajau people of Southeast Asia live in stilt houses,
and can fish underwater for up to five minutes on one breath.
This poem was inspired by one such freediving fisherman called
Sulbin, who was filmed by the BBC for their Human Planet
series as he hunted in the ocean off the east coast of Sabah, Borneo.*

Ariel's Song

WILLIAM SHAKESPEARE

Full fathom five thy father lies;
Of his bones are coral made;
Those are pearls that were his eyes:
Nothing of him that doth fade,
But doth suffer a sea-change
Into something rich and strange.
Sea-nymphs hourly ring his knell:

                              Ding-dong.

Hark! now I hear them, – ding-dong, bell.

Community Rain Song

OODGEROO NOONUCCAL (KATH WALKER)

At the old tribal squatting-place
Behind the camp gunyas
Tonight they were doing their Wyambi rain song
Under the bright stars.
This was nardoo-gathering season
But now little nardoo. Too long dry,
Grass all brown, birds not breeding,
Creeks not running, clouds gone long time.
This is not a ritual secret and sacred,
This is a camp game, a community playabout,
Even some of the women there, even the children.
But some of the old men aloof and grave
Throughout all the laughter muttered strange words
Of magic-making as old as the race,
Handed down through countless generations,
Not understood now but faithfully repeated,
Lost rain-words from ancestral times.
Behind the bushes sounded
The weird whirring drone of the dread bullroarer,
While all waited motionless
As a great figure-group carved in stone

Dim in the firelight.

Now into view with dance steps advancing
A line of painted song-men
Chanting in unison:
'Rain come down!
Rain come down!'
And the squatting horde in chorus:
'Rain come down!'
'Creek run soon!
Creek run soon!
You great sky ones, fill dry waterhole,
Send rain down!'
'Creek run soon!
Send rain down!'

'Rainbird come,
That fellow know, he talk and tell us
Rain fall down!'
At once the whole Wyambi people
Took up the loud toneless scream
Of the giant cuckoo they called the rainbird
Whose coming always predicted rain.
A rhythm of 'Rain fall down!' mingled
With the harsh calls of the bird.

'*Frog talk now,*
Wake up now,
Frog fellow singing out, they telling all about
Rain come down!'
Joyously then the tribe came in
With the croaking of frogs little and big,
Filling a swamp with bedlam of joy
At the nearness of rain:
'Wark, awark, wark!'
'Eek, eek, cree-eek!'
'Ork! Ork!'

'*Plover here now,*
Plover loud now,
He sure rain-bringer, he tell blackfellow
Rain fall down!'
From all the rows of people now
Came perfectly the spurwinged plover's sharp
Excited staccato:
'Karra-karak!'
'Keerk-keerk!'
'Karaka-karra-karak!'

'*Wind he come,*
Little wind first time.

He say soon big blow follow him
And rain fall down!'
'Wee-oo, whoo-oo!' came the wail of the wind,
'Whish-awhee-ee!'
'Awhoo-whoo!'

'Thunder up there,
Rumble up there,
Dooloomai the Thunderer he tumble all about,
Shake rain down!'
Like answer came a deep rolling thunder
From the men, while the women with open palms
Beat rapidly upon skin rugs
Stretched taut between their knees like drums
Till the hollow sound
Swelled to a loud booming and then
Gradually died away.

'Rain come down! Rain come down!'
Chorused the line of dancers, threw
Into the air handfuls of water
From bark yorlis as they stamped and swayed,
Chanting
The repetitions of the rain song,
While from the ranked Wyambis rose

The toneless monotone of showers,
Hard to do and done superbly –
Leafy boughs, rattling gravel, voices, all
Blended as one to reproduce
The universal sound of steady rain.

The tempo increased, all the rain symbols now
Mingled in pandemonium. Frogs croaked,
Rainbird screamed, thunder rolled,
The rising whine of wind
Cut across cries of plover, and
As the background to it all
The deep steady drumming of the rain:
'Wark, awark-wark!'
'Wee-whoo-awhoo!'
'Karra-karak-karak!'
'Boom! Bombomba-oom-m-m!'
'Cree-eek! Ork! Ork!'
'Whish-awhee-ee!'
'Rain come down! Rain come down!'
It looked like going on half the night.
A dingo on a low ridge
Half a mile away
Stood motionless with pricked ears looking down
On the strange goings-on below, dim-lit

By the dying Wyambi fires. These
Were the feared and hated men-creatures
Nothing in all the bush could understand.
He turned away into the dark.

Down on the squatting-place,
Lost in the merry-making, no one marked
That rising of a little wind
That rustled the belahs and then began
To sway them; none saw
That the clear stars above them had disappeared.

Suddenly
A blinding white fork of lightning
Stood for an instant close above them
And instantaneously
A double shattering crash of thunder
That shook the world. All sprang up
Laughing and screaming,
Half in terror and half in joy as the first
Slow drops of rain began to fall; the wind
Whipped up to a gale and whooped about them,
Sparks from the fires
Went whirled in showers across the dark
As the rain roared to a downpour.

'*The caves! The caves!*'
Some snatched up firesticks and in a straggling line
The excited Wyambi people
Went streaming off along the empty creek
Towards the great red caves of sandstone where
They sheltered at night in the worst wet weather.
Oi! Oi! Good playabout that time!
Oi! Oi! A night to be remembered.

Rain on Dry Ground

CHRISTOPHER FRY

That is rain on dry ground. We heard it:
We saw the little tempest in the ground,
The panic of anticipation: heard
The uneasy leaves flutter, The air pass
In a wave, the fluster of the vegetation:

Head the first spatter of drops, the outriders
Larruping on the road, hitting against
The gate of the drought, and shattering
On to the lances of the tottering meadow
It is rain; It is rain on dry ground.

Rain riding suddenly out of the air
Battering the bare walls of the sun.
It is falling on the lounge of the blackbird,
Into the heart of the thrush; the dazed valley
Sings it down. Rain, rain on dry ground!

This the urgent decision of the day,
The urgent drubbing of earth, the urgent raid
On the dust; downpour over the flaring poppy,

Deluge on the face of noon, the flagellent
Rain drenching across the air. The day

Flows in the ditch; bubble and twisting twig
And the sudden morning swirl along together
Under the crying hedge. And where the sun
Ran on the scythes, the rain runs down
The obliterated field, the blunted crop.

The rain stops,
The air is sprung with green.
The intercepted drops
Fall at their leisure; and between
The threading runnels on the slopes
The snail drags his caution into the sun.

Waterfall Haiku

MATSUO BASHŌ

Translated from the Japanese by R. H. Blythe

A clear waterfall;
Into the ripples
Fall green pine-needles.

A Green Land Full of Rivers

SABRINA MAHFOUZ

A green land full of rivers
and warm-to-the-touch rain,
my Grandad said the drops washed away the pain
your legs used to feel after mama give you a lickin',
but even the ocean couldn't soothe the sting
of papa's cruel words, he knew just how to pick them.

Shipped over from Madeira to work sugar fields,
once his dad saw his mum,
he knew his fate was sealed.
She was of the forest, he was of the sea –
but in Guyana, it'd be okay, and it was.
They got married on a steamy,
sticky jungle day in May.

Him and his Chinese friend set up
the best Roti stall in town,
it did so well that once a month
he bought his wife a sparkly gown.
All the women would cut their eyes
and look and stare,

shouting at their man –
why ya kna buy me dat, I want dat, it no fair!

So the women danced with her man,
jealous for what she had,
and he was no better, dancing right back.
Frustrated by feeling inferior,
she took it out on my Grandad.
Locked him alone for days in a dark room,
with just a thin stick of sugar cane,
my Grandad prayed for her to be happy,
but the day never came.

His father spoke of England –
it was rich and grand and fair,
he spoke of it with deep-felt love –
though he'd never, ever been there.
At the age of eighteen,
Grandad buried his father and boarded a ship,
he was going to England
with just a sugar cane stick in his pocket –

it would be a long trip.

Mail Drop

PAUL CAMERON BROWN

A boat sits on the very shallows
of a lake
in egg-cup fashion,
a tea-cosy covering waves,
orchestrating the bob of colours
in white enamel blue
inverted water.

Afar, the boat is a rasher of bacon
a strip, stripling, stipend
slicing the lake,
distancing.

The boat is an envelope
at the end of the world,
planet-sized, pea-green
about to spin crazily
into the sun at the
end of a rifle-sized
mail drop.

The boat rides amid the
between places of things,
furtive longings
where crones sit within
waiting bushes &
lizards visit skin,
dirge of teeth gnashing
the fringe canopy of
flowing leaves.

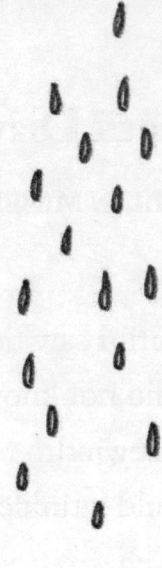

Until I Saw the Sea

LILIAN MOORE

Until I saw the sea
I did not know
that wind
could wrinkle water so.

I never knew
that sun
could splinter a whole sea of blue.

Nor
did I know before,
a sea breathes in and out
upon a shore.

A View of the Han River

WANG WEI

Translated from the Chinese by Witter Bynner and Kiang Kang-hu

With its three Hsiang branches it reaches the Chu
   border,
And with nine streams touches the gateway of Ching:
This river runs beyond heaven and earth,
Where the colour of mountains both is and is not.
The dwellings of men seem floating along
On ripples of the distant sky—
Oh Hsiang-yang, how your beautiful days
Make drunken my old mountain-heart!

The Poet and the Brook

JULIANA HORATIA EWING

A little Brook, that babbled under grass,
Once saw a Poet pass—
A Poet with long hair and saddened eyes,
Who went his weary way with woeful sighs.
And on another time,
This Brook did hear that Poet read his rueful rhyme.
Now in the poem that he read,
This Poet said—
"Oh! little Brook that babblest under grass!
(*Ah me! Alack! Ah, well-a-day! Alas!*)
Say, are you what you seem?
Or is your life, like other lives, a dream?
What time your babbling mocks my mortal moods,
Fair of the stream!
And are you, in good sooth,
Could purblind poesy perceive the truth,
A water-sprite,
Who sometimes, for man's dangerous delight,
Puts on a human form and face,
To wear them with a superhuman grace?

Song of the Rain

KHALIL GIBRAN

I am dotted silver threads dropped from heaven
By the gods. Nature then takes me, to adorn
Her fields and valleys.

I am beautiful pearls, plucked from the
Crown of Ishtar by the daughter of Dawn
To embellish the gardens.

When I cry the hills laugh;
When I humble myself the flowers rejoice;
When I bow, all things are elated.

The field and the cloud are lovers
And between them I am a messenger of mercy.
I quench the thirst of one;
I cure the ailment of the other.

The voice of thunder declares my arrival;
The rainbow announces my departure.
I am like earthly life, which begins at

The feet of the mad elements and ends
Under the upraised wings of death.

I emerge from the heard of the sea
Soar with the breeze. When I see a field in
Need, I descend and embrace the flowers and
The trees in a million little ways.

I touch gently at the windows with my
Soft fingers, and my announcement is a
Welcome song. All can hear, but only
The sensitive can understand.

The heat in the air gives birth to me,
But in turn I kill it,
As woman overcomes man with
The strength she takes from him.

I am the sigh of the sea;
The laughter of the field;
The tears of heaven.

So with love –
Sighs from the deep sea of affection;

Laughter from the colourful field of the spirit;
Tears from the endless heaven of memories.

The Woodpecker

ELIZABETH MADOX ROBERTS

The woodpecker pecked out a little round hole
And made him a house in the telephone pole.
One day when I watched he poked out his head,
And he had on a hood and a collar of red.

When the streams of rain pour out of the sky,
And the sparkles of lightning go flashing by,
And the big, big wheels of thunder roll,
He can snuggle back in the telephone pole.

A Sea-Song

SOPHIE M. HENSLEY

A dash of spray,
A weed-browned way, –
My ship's in the bay,
In the glad blue bay, –
The wind's from the west
And the waves have a crest,
But my bird's in the nest
And my ship's in the bay!

At dawn to stand
Soft hand to hand,
Bare feet on the sand, –
On the hard brown sand, –
To wait, dew-crowned,
For the tarrying sound
Of a keel that will ground
On the scraping sand.

A glad surprise
In the wind-swept skies
Of my wee one's eyes, –

Those wondering eyes.
He will come, my sweet,
And will haste to meet
Those hurrying feet
And those sea-blue eyes.

I know the day
Must weary away,
And my ship's in the bay, –
In the clear, blue bay, –
Ah! there's wind in the west,
For the waves have a crest,
But my bird's in the nest
And my ship's in the bay!

Little Fish

D. H. LAWRENCE

The tiny fish enjoy themselves
in the sea.
Quick little splinters of life,
their little lives are fun to them
in the sea.

Big Swimming

EDWIN FORD PIPER

Rain on the high prairies,
In dusk of autumnal hills;
Under the creaking saddle
My cheerless pony plods…

Down where the obscure water
Lapping the lithe willows
Sunders the chilling plain –
Rusty-hearted and travel-worn –
We set our bodies
To the November flood.

The farther shore is a cloud
Beyond midnight…

Big swimming.

Rainfall

EMILY PAULINE JOHNSON

From out the west, where darkling storm-clouds float,
The waking wind pipes soft its rising note.

From out the west, o'erhung with fringes grey,
The wind preludes with sighs its roundelay,

Then blowing, singing, piping, laughing loud,
It scurries on before the grey storm-cloud;

Across the hollow and along the hill
It whips and whirls among the maples, till

With boughs upbent, and green of leaves blown wide,
The silver shines upon their underside.

A gusty freshening of humid air,
With showers laden, and with fragrance rare;

And now a little sprinkle, with a dash
Of great cool drops that fall with sudden splash;

Then over field and hollow, grass and grain,
The loud, crisp whiteness of the nearing rain.

Weather Proverb

ANONYMOUS

Mackerel sky, mackerel sky…
Never long wet, never long dry.

From Wet Weather Talk

JAMES WHITCOMB RILEY

It hain't no use to grumble and complane;
It's jest as cheap and easy to rejoice.—
When God sorts out the weather and sends rain,
W'y, rain's my choice.

The Crocodile

LEWIS CARROLL

How doth the little crocodile
   Improve his shining tail,
And pour the waters of the Nile
   On every golden scale!

How cheerfully he seems to grin,
   How neatly spreads his claws,
And welcomes little fishes in,
   With gently smiling jaws!

Beachcomber

GEORGE MACKAY BROWN

Monday I found a boot –
Rust and salt leather.
I gave it back to the sea, to dance in.

Tuesday a spar of timber worth thirty bob.
Next winter
It will be a chair, a coffin, a bed.

Wednesday a half can of Swedish spirits.
I tilted my head.
The shore was cold with mermaids and angels.

Thursday I got nothing, seaweed,
A whale bone,
Wet feet and a loud cough.

Friday I held a seaman's skull,
Sand spilling from it
The way time is told on kirkyard stones.

Saturday a barrel of sodden oranges.
A Spanish ship
Was wrecked last month at The Kame.

Sunday, for fear of the elders,
I sit on my bum.
What's heaven? A sea chest with a thousand gold coins.

The Deserted House

MARY COLERIDGE

There's no smoke in the chimney,
And the rain beats on the floor;
There's no glass in the window,
There's no wood in the door;
The heather grows behind the house,
And the sand lies before.

No hand hath trained the ivy,
The walls are grey and bare;
The boats upon the sea sail by,
Nor ever tarry there.
No beast of the field comes nigh,
Nor any bird of the air.

Wynken, Blynken, and Nod

EUGENE FIELD

Wynken, Blynken, and Nod one night
    Sailed off in a wooden shoe—
Sailed on a river of crystal light,
    Into a sea of dew.
"Where are you going, and what do you wish?"
    The old moon asked of the three.
"We have come to fish for the herring fish
That live in this beautiful sea;
Nets of silver and gold have we!"
      Said Wynken,
      Blynken,
      And Nod.

The old moon laughed and sang a song,
    As they rocked in the wooden shoe,
And the wind that sped them all night long
    Ruffled the waves of dew.
The little stars were the herring fish
    That lived in that beautiful sea—
"Now cast your nets wherever you wish—
    Never afeard are we!"

So cried the stars to the fishermen three:
    Wynken,
    Blynken,
    And Nod.

All night long their nets they threw
    To the stars in the twinkling foam—
Then down from the skies came the wooden shoe,
    Bringing the fishermen home;
'Twas all so pretty a sail it seemed
    As if it could not be,
And some folks thought 'twas a dream they'd dreamed
    Of sailing that beautiful sea—
    But I shall name you the fishermen three:
    Wynken,
    Blynken,
    And Nod.

Wynken and Blynken are two little eyes,
    And Nod is a little head,
And the wooden shoe that sailed the skies
    Is a wee one's trundle-bed.
So shut your eyes while mother sings
    Of wonderful sights that be,
And you shall see the beautiful things

As you rock in the misty sea,
Where the old shoe rocked the fishermen three:
Wynken,
Blynken,
And Nod.

Dancing

YANG KUEI-FEI

Wide sleeves sway.
Scents,
Sweet scents
Incessantly coming.
It is red lilies,
Lotus lilies,
Floating up,
And up,
Out of Autumn mist.
Thin clouds
Puffed,
Fluttered,
Blown on a rippling wind
Through a mountain pass.
Young willow shoots
Touching,
Brushing,
The water
Of the garden pool.

The Maldive Shark

HERMAN MELVILLE

About the Shark, phlegmatical one,
Pale sot of the Maldive sea,
The sleek little pilot-fish, azure and slim,
How alert in attendance be.
From his saw-pit of mouth, from his charnel of maw
They have nothing of harm to dread,
But liquidly glide on his ghastly flank
Or before his Gorgonian head;
Or lurk in the port of serrated teeth
In white triple tiers of glittering gates,
And there find a haven when peril's abroad,
An asylum in jaws of the Fates!
They are friends; and friendly they guide him to prey,
Yet never partake of the treat—
Eyes and brains to the dotard lethargic and dull,
Pale ravener of horrible meat.

The Tide Rises, the Tide Falls

HENRY WADSWORTH LONGFELLOW

The tide rises, the tide falls,
The twilight darkens, the curlew calls;
Along the sea-sands damp and brown
The traveller hastens toward the town,
    And the tide rises, the tide falls.

Darkness settles on roofs and walls,
But the sea, the sea in the darkness calls;
The little waves, with their soft, white hands,
Efface the footprints in the sands,
    And the tide rises, the tide falls.

The morning breaks; the steeds in their stalls
Stamp and neigh, as the hostler calls;
The day returns, but nevermore
Returns the traveller to the shore,
    And the tide rises, the tide falls.

Duck's Ditty

KENNETH GRAHAME

All along the backwater,
Through the rushes tall,
Ducks are a-dabbling,
Up tails all!

Ducks' tails, drakes' tails,
Yellow feet a-quiver,
Yellow bills all out of sight
Busy in the river!

Slushy green undergrowth
Where the roach swim—
Here we keep our larder,
Cool and full and dim.

Everyone for what he likes!
We like to be
Heads down, tails up,
Dabbling free!

High in the blue above
Swifts whirl and call—
We are down a-dabbling
Up tails all!

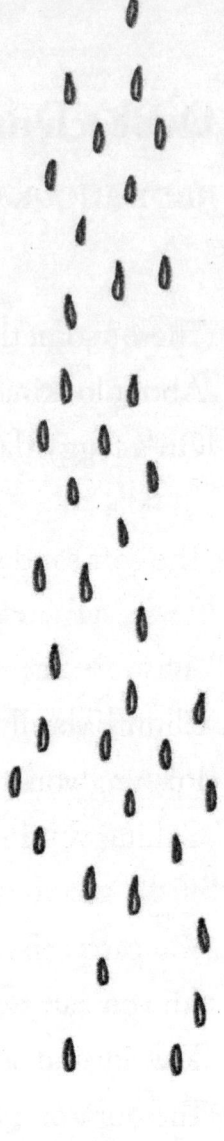

A Beach on a Foggy Day

JADE ANOUKA

There's something truly magical
About looking out from a beach
On a foggy day.

The soft sand sinking beneath your shoes
As the waves kiss
And retract from you
Calling you in
Pushing you away
Calling you in again.

You can't see how far you can see
All you can see is sky
The sky and sea as one
The horizon nowhere.

You look around
You're in a perfect bubble of air
All around is water
You can taste it
The sea or the sky or both.

The mystery of what's beyond
Sings to you
Enticing you into a dream
A day dream
A dream of what's out there
Inside the fog
Beyond the sea

Creatures fly into it
Others fly back
Changed?
They've been where you wish to
The mysterious space
Beyond the fog
Beyond the sea
Where the horizon must be.

That magical place you want to see
So far away
When looking out from a beach
On a foggy day.

From The Scallop Shell

DORA SIGERSON SHORTER

A scallop shell, loosed by the lifting tide,
    Had left a friendly shore, the seas to brave;
   Its lips of pink and snowy hollow shone
    Pure in the sun, a pearl upon the wave.

Little Raindrops

JANE EUPHEMIA BROWNE

Oh, where do you come from,
You little drops of rain,
Pitter patter, pitter patter,
Down the window pane?

They won't let me walk,
And they won't let me play,
And they won't let me go
Out of doors at all today.

They put away my playthings.
Because I broke them all,
And then they locked up all my bricks,
And took away my ball.

Tell me, little raindrops,
Is that the way you play,
Pitter patter, pitter patter,
All the rainy day?

They say I'm very naughty,
But I've nothing else to do
But sit here at the window;
I should like to play with you.

The little raindrops cannot speak,
But 'pitter patter pat'
Means, "We can play on this side,
Why can't you play on that?"

Tsunami

JOYDEB AND MOYNA CHITRAKAR

Translated from the Bengali by
Mala Chakraborthy and Sirish Rao

Lend me your ears now
Hear out my words now
The tragic story that I sing
Of the wave that took everything
Tsunami!
Swallower of the living

It was two thousand four
Before the year closed its door
Tragedy struck all things dear
Fate's hand touched us here
Tsunami!
Water-quake of fear

Drowned here, drowned there
Things under water everywhere
Ships, houses, trains on rails
Nothing escapes the watery trail
When death falls thick and fast

Fame and fortune, nothing lasts
Tsunami!
You made present things past

Reporters arrive: eyes of the world
Across all nations the story is told
As people watch in horror on TV
Tsunami!
The swallowing sea

A girl floats by, clutching a door
No friends, no parents any more
Tears well in my eyes again
Unmourned deaths, all in vain
Tsunami!
Who spread such pain

But not all fall prey to the sea
Animals sense it coming and flee
To take refuge on mountain tops
Where the water's tongue is
finally chopped
Tsunami!
Who cannot be stopped

Helicopters fly, relief rains down
People fighting for food in village and town
Is this destiny, to die like flies?
I cannot stop the tears that fill my eyes
Help and politics and petty tricks
Go hand in hand amongst the broken bricks
How much more can hungry people take?
Tsunami!
You water-quake

And in all this suffering, some things to take pride
Hindus and Muslims are buried side by side
In the graveyard of a mosque, now open to all
Religious walls for a moment, fall
Tsunami!
Who hurt us all

Another story of hope before I go:
An old temple stands on the shore
That has seen much come and go
Will it fall to the water's tongue?
Will its song no more be sung?

But no!

It endures the crashing gales
And a hidden temple by its side
the water unveils
Revealed by the waves that ate the sand
Even in destruction, you showed something grand

Tsunami!
You thief of land

The Sea

BARRY CORNWALL

THE SEA! the sea! the open sea!
The blue, the fresh, the ever free!
Without a mark, without a bound,
It runneth the earth's wide regions round;
It plays with the clouds; it mocks the skies;
Or like a cradled creature lies.

I'm on the sea! I'm on the sea!
I am where I would ever be;
With the blue above, and the blue below,
And silence wheresoe'er I go;
If a storm should come and awake the deep,
What matter? I shall ride and sleep.

I love, O, how I love to ride
On the fierce, foaming, bursting tide,
When every mad wave drowns the moon
Or whistles aloft his tempest tune,
And tells how goeth the world below,
And why the sou'west blasts do blow.

I never was on the dull, tame shore,
But I lov'd the great sea more and more,
And backwards flew to her billowy breast,
Like a bird that seeketh its mother's nest;
And a mother she was, and is, to me;
For I was born on the open sea!
The waves were white, and red the morn,

In the noisy hour when I was born;
And the whale it whistled, the porpoise roll'd,
And the dolphins bared their backs of gold;
And never was heard such an outcry wild
As welcom'd to life the ocean-child!

I've liv'd since then, in calm and strife,
Full fifty summers, a sailor's life,
With wealth to spend and a power to range,
But never have sought nor sighed for change;
And Death, whenever he comes to me,
Shall come on the wild, unbounded sea!

Laguna

PRATYUSHA

the ocean turns green algae into light,
swallows its green, washes its own memory.

the ocean braids its hair, sadness split
into three.

August brushing
my hands like palm fronds.

when the monsoon comes, the trees
loosen their braids, sing the wind's sorrows

into water. all of this water, the sadness of
a knowledge.

slip your shadow into the sea.
drag silt from your own mouth.

The Jumblies

EDWARD LEAR

I

They went to sea in a Sieve, they did,
    In a Sieve they went to sea:
In spite of all their friends could say,
On a winter's morn, on a stormy day,
    In a Sieve they went to sea!
And when the Sieve turned round and round,
And every one cried, 'You'll all be drowned!'
They called aloud, 'Our Sieve ain't big,
But we don't care a button! we don't care a fig!
    In a Sieve we'll go to sea!'
      Far and few, far and few,
        Are the lands where the Jumblies live;
        Their heads are green, and their hands are blue,
        And they went to sea in a Sieve.

II

They sailed away in a Sieve, they did,
   In a Sieve they sailed so fast,
With only a beautiful pea-green veil
Tied with a riband by way of a sail,
   To a small tobacco-pipe mast;
And every one said, who saw them go,
'O won't they be soon upset, you know!
For the sky is dark, and the voyage is long,
And happen what may, it's extremely wrong
   In a Sieve to sail so fast!'
     Far and few, far and few,
       Are the lands where the Jumblies live;
       Their heads are green, and their hands are blue,
       And they went to sea in a Sieve.

III

The water it soon came in, it did,
   The water it soon came in;
So to keep them dry, they wrapped their feet
In a pinky paper all folded neat,
   And they fastened it down with a pin.
And they passed the night in a crockery-jar,

And each of them said, 'How wise we are!
Though the sky be dark, and the voyage be long,
Yet we never can think we were rash or wrong,
    While round in our Sieve we spin!'
        Far and few, far and few,
            Are the lands where the Jumblies live;
            Their heads are green, and their hands are blue,
            And they went to sea in a Sieve.

IV

And all night long they sailed away;
    And when the sun went down,
They whistled and warbled a moony song
To the echoing sound of a coppery gong,
    In the shade of the mountains brown.
'O Timballo! How happy we are,
When we live in a sieve and a crockery-jar,
And all night long in the moonlight pale,
We sail away with a pea-green sail,
    In the shade of the mountains brown!'
        Far and few, far and few,
            Are the lands where the Jumblies live;
            Their heads are green, and their hands are blue,
            And they went to sea in a Sieve.

V

They sailed to the Western Sea, they did,
  To a land all covered with trees,
And they bought an Owl, and a useful Cart,
And a pound of Rice, and a Cranberry Tart,
  And a hive of silvery Bees.
And they bought a Pig, and some green Jack-daws,
And a lovely Monkey with lollipop paws,
And forty bottles of Ring-Bo-Ree,
  And no end of Stilton Cheese.
    Far and few, far and few,
      Are the lands where the Jumblies live;
      Their heads are green, and their hands are blue,
      And they went to sea in a Sieve.

VI

And in twenty years they all came back,
  In twenty years or more,
And every one said, 'How tall they've grown!'
For they've been to the Lakes, and the Torrible Zone,
  And the hills of the Chankly Bore;
And they drank their health, and gave them a feast
Of dumplings made of beautiful yeast;

And everyone said, 'If we only live,
We too will go to sea in a Sieve,—
To the hills of the Chankly Bore!'
Far and few, far and few,
Are the lands where the Jumblies live;
Their heads are green, and their hands are blue,
And they went to sea in a Sieve.

Ghazal with Rain and Birds

SHAZEA QURAISHI

Day opens its eyes: sky's pillowed with cloud.
Each morning's a gift, a melody bright with birds.

Rain is beginning, and rain is ending,
longed-for and sudden, as heavy, as light as birds.

A tree is a village, a garden, a town,
a thunder of wingbeats, a day and a night of birds.

Streets freshly watered, a telephone line
is strung as if pearled, with white after white after white
    bird.

The breeze brings a kite painted with flowers -
it's caught in the arms of the tree, alight with birds.

Come to the river, to its bed full of stones,
Come rest on the green of its bank, a delight for birds.

A Ghazal is a form of poem or ode, originating in Arabic poetry.
It is generally used to express a feeling of love, or longing, or separation.

Sea Fever

JOHN MASEFIELD

I must go down to the seas again, to the lonely sea and
    the sky,
And all I ask is a tall ship and a star to steer her by;
And the wheel's kick and the wind's song and the white
    sail's shaking,
And a grey mist on the sea's face, and a grey dawn
    breaking.

I must go down to the seas again, for the call of the
    running tide
Is a wild call and a clear call that may not be denied;
And all I ask is a windy day with the white clouds
    flying,
And the flung spray and the blown spume, and the
    sea-gulls crying.

I must go down to the seas again, to the vagrant gypsy
    life,
To the gull's way and the whale's way where the wind's
    like a whetted knife;
And all I ask is a merry yarn from a laughing
    fellow-rover,
And quiet sleep and a sweet dream when the long
    trick's over.

Dover Beach

MATTHEW ARNOLD

The sea is calm tonight.
The tide is full, the moon lies fair
Upon the straits; on the French coast the light
Gleams and is gone; the cliffs of England stand,
Glimmering and vast, out in the tranquil bay.
Come to the window, sweet is the night-air!
Only, from the long line of spray
Where the sea meets the moon-blanched land,
Listen! you hear the grating roar
Of pebbles which the waves draw back, and fling,
At their return, up the high strand,
Begin, and cease, and then again begin,
With tremulous cadence slow, and bring
The eternal note of sadness in.

Sophocles long ago
Heard it on the Ægean, and it brought
Into his mind the turbid ebb and flow
Of human misery; we
Find also in the sound a thought,
Hearing it by this distant northern sea.

The Sea of Faith
Was once, too, at the full, and round earth's shore
Lay like the folds of a bright girdle furled.
But now I only hear
Its melancholy, long, withdrawing roar,
Retreating, to the breath
Of the night-wind, down the vast edges drear
And naked shingles of the world.

Ah, love, let us be true
To one another! for the world, which seems
To lie before us like a land of dreams,
So various, so beautiful, so new,
Hath really neither joy, nor love, nor light,
Nor certitude, nor peace, nor help for pain;
And we are here as on a darkling plain
Swept with confused alarms of struggle and flight,
Where ignorant armies clash by night.

Puddle

KATE TEMPEST

It was a grey old day, it looked like rain
But you were laughing all the same
We went off to the climbing frame
You couldn't wait to play!

All wrapped up in waterproofs
Your favourite bright red welly boots
You wobbled like a wobbly tooth
As we made our way.

Off to the park, off to the swings
Like two kites in the bouncing wind
You held my hand and jumped and jumped
Right way up, then back to front.

You skipped over the cracks and bumps
Hello! said the cat curled up on the ledge
From paving stone to paving stone
Hello! Said the beetle curled up in the hedge.

Then you saw it! You stopped walking
Clapped your hands and jumped for joy
Looked back at me to check I'd seen
The greatest best most perfect toy –

A puddle!

You slid your toes around the edge,
Then sunk your ankles in
Started stamping up and down
Your face a muddy grin.
I couldn't believe
You had mud on your knees
Mud on your sleeves,
Mud on your chin!

Oh no! I shouted. Out you get!
But before I could speak another word
I heard a sound and looked around
As something very strange occurred:

All the houses on the street
Blinked their lights and swished their blinds
And all the letterboxes flapped
And all the fenceposts danced in line!

The trees by the pond pulled up their roots
And stamped their ancient toes
And made a big old wave so tall
It rose and rose and rose.

And all the ducks went surfing
High up into the air
To look through the top deck bus windows
At all the people there.

Look! They quacked, and pointed down
As you splashed in the street
And all the people off to work
Were dancing in their seats!

EARTH SPINS

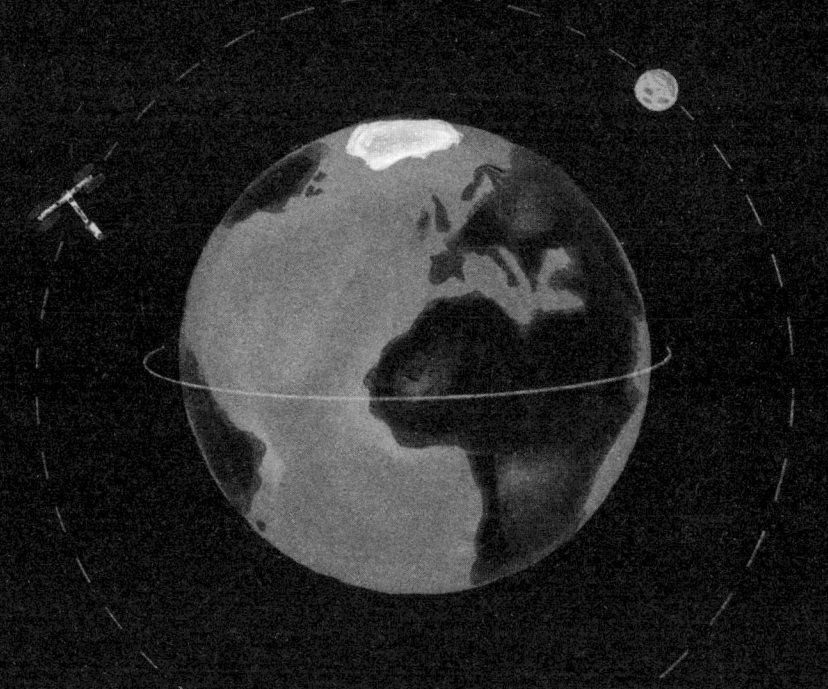

AROUND AND AROUND
AND NEVER MAKES A SPINNING
SOUND...

The Spinning Earth

AILEEN FISHER

The earth, they say,
spins round and round.
It doesn't look it from the ground,
and never makes a spinning sound.
And water never swirls and swishes
from oceans full of dizzy fishes,
and shelves don't lose their pans and dishes.
And houses don't go whirling by,
or puppies swirl around the sky,
or robins spin instead of fly.
It may be true what people say
about one spinning night and day…
but I keep wondering, anyway.

Mother
(after Elizabeth Barrett Browning)

OAKLEY FLANAGAN

'Bad world,' the newspapers print. 'Bad, bad world.'
'Sad day,' the adults say. 'Such a sad, sad day.'

But louder than the adult's pessimism, the child
sings 'Hope' – Nature's ancient rabble cry.

In Mother Nature's garden live her *generations of birds*
& a child tending rose-buds, mindful of the thorn-
    bush.

Flocks of birds above, singing,
singing louder than the *sighing*.

The child is the gate-keeper of Mother Nature's greatest
    gift.
How its chorus rouse soars, higher than the adult's
    cynicism.

Flying way up, feathered wings out –
stretched, keeping the sky upright.

Whilst we below –
look up to marvel

at its rich loop of flight. Song: the condition
of the good gardener, ever-watchful of the bird

who never stops its song to wonder if it's being heard.
The bird makes itself known by singing, on & on.

Reminding us down here, it is the earth we spring from.
Earth eternally –

Like age-old waves, carrying history in its lap.
The constant splash of waves, waves breaking,

coming back. Stormy nights may feel never ending,
but when morning's melody wakes you, half asleep,

it heralds a new day with kinder colours up ahead,
keeping faith in nature. Return to Mother's garden –

Listen to the winds of Change. Watch Time sweep.
Land transform. Mother watching us silently,

seeing all. This is her gift to us, for us to cherish
with our time, our care, our love.

See the unending stars *in their old glory*,
just as they've always shone. The Moon & The Sun,

old loves in happy union, lighting each day & night
& Mother, who brought us into this world, asks but one
    thing of us

Remember what you are from –

Quiet magic: the empathy a cooling dock-leaf can
    teach.
The humility an acorn must learn, before it can become
    a tree.

The generosity of a daffodil; its abundant yellow hue, a
    tiny sun
shines brightly when unpicked, for other's joy in
    glimpsing it too.

Look! How it seems to erupt from the deepest part of
    ground,
Mother's ancient lore of family resounds. All of us but
    blades of grass

changing seasonally. Growing together, *contended*,
  through sun, sleet or snow,
there are no weeds here – not really – that's what the
  good gardener knows.

No matter how much the winds decline, or the
  lightening brings us toil,
'We are all flowers, all of us,' she reminds. 'Flowers of the
  self-same soil.'

The Worm

RALPH BERGENGREN

When the earth is turned in spring
The worms are fat as anything.

And birds come flying all around
To eat the worms right off the ground.

They like the worms just as much as I
Like bread and milk and apple pie.

And once, when I was very young,
I put a worm right on my tongue.

I didn't like the taste a bit,
And so I didn't swallow it.

But oh, it makes my Mother squirm
Because she *thinks* I ate that worm!

Counting-Out Rhyme

EDNA ST. VINCENT MILLAY

Silver bark of beech, and sallow
Bark of yellow birch and yellow
  Twig of willow.

Stripe of green in moosewood maple,
Colour seen in leaf of apple,
  Bark of popple.

Wood of popple pale as moonbeam,
Wood of oak for yoke and barn-beam,
  Wood of hornbeam.

Silver bark of beech, and hollow
Stem of elder, tall and yellow
  Twig of willow.

From Childe Harold's Pilgrimage

LORD BYRON

There is pleasure in the pathless woods
There is rapture in the lonely shore,
There is society where none intrudes,
By the deep Sea, and music in its roar;
I love not Man the less, but Nature more.

Enjoy the Earth

TRADITIONAL YORUBA

Enjoy the earth gently
Enjoy the earth gently
For if the earth is spoiled
It cannot be repaired
Enjoy the earth gently.

Pleasant Sounds

JOHN CLARE

The rustling of leaves under the feet in woods and
under hedges;

The crumpling of cat-ice and snow down wood-rides,
narrow lanes, and every street causeway;

Rustling through a wood or rather rushing, while the
wind halloos in the oak-toop like thunder;

The rustle of birds' wings startled from their nests or
flying unseen into the bushes;

The whizzing of larger birds overhead in a wood, such
as crows, puddocks, buzzards;

The trample of robins and woodlarks on the brown
leaves, and the patter of squirrels on the green moss;

The fall of an acorn on the ground, the pattering of nuts
on the hazel branches as they fall from ripeness;

The flirt of the groundlark's wing from the stubbles–
how sweet such pictures on dewy mornings, when the
dew flashes from its brown feathers.

Epigram for the Bald

ANONYMOUS

Translated from the Latin by Sabrina Mahfouz

Leaves return to trees,

Grass regrows on the ground:

But not one hair on your bald head is to be found!

Song

PAUL LAURENCE DUNBAR

A bee that was searching for sweets one day
Through the gate of a rose garden happened to stray.
In the heart of a rose he hid away,
And forgot in his bliss the light of day,
As sipping his honey he buzzed in song;
Though day was waning, he lingered long,
For the rose was sweet, so sweet.

A robin sits pluming his ruddy breast,
And a madrigal sings to his love in her nest:
"Oh, the skies they are blue, the fields are green,
And the birds in your nest will soon be seen!"
She hangs on his words with a thrill of love,
And chirps to him as he sits above
For the song is sweet, so sweet.

A maiden was out on a summer's day
With the winds and the waves and the flowers at play;
And she met with a youth of gentle air,
With the light of the sunshine on his hair.
Together they wandered the flowers among;

They loved, and loving they lingered long,
For to love is sweet, so sweet.

Laverton Incident

JACK DAVIS

The two worlds collided
In anger and fear
As it has always been –
Gun against spear.

Aboriginal earth,
Hungry and dry,
Took back the life again,
Wondering why.

Echo the gun-blast
Throughout the land
Before more blood seeps
Into the sand.

Autumn Evening

MATSUO BASHŌ

Translated from the Japanese by Kenneth Rexroth

Autumn evening –
A crow on a bare branch.

At Night I Talk to the Giant's Finger

STEPHEN LIGHTBOWN

We walk through the woods near my house
on the way to the supermarket.
I count 100 trees.

Some tall, some small,
some green, others lean.
All strong, very steady.

They always know I am coming.
I ask them what they see.
I put my hand on the bark

of my favourite – it feels rough
like the scab on my forehead
from when I fell in the playground.

Mum took me to the hospital.
They stuck my head back together
with sticky sap glue.

I kneel on the ground and stretch my fingers
into the dark soil like roots. The mud is cold and wet.
No wonder the trees wear thick green moss socks.

When I'm tucked up in bed.
When everything is still and silent.
When sleep is far away.

I wait.
I wait.
I wait.

For the tap tap tap at my window.

Tap tap.
Tap tap.
Tap tap.

I climb over shadows onto the window sill
    and draw back my curtains to see
a branch as long as a giant's arm

slowly tapping the window
to let me know it's there, that I'm safe.

It knows because the other trees
have whispered through the ground

I was in the woods today.

The Shadow of a Tree

WEST AFRICAN PROVERB

When the shadow of a tree is curved,
straighten the tree,
not the shadow.

Once Upon a Time

MARY E. WILKINS FREEMAN

Now, once upon a time, a nest of fairies
Was in a meadow 'neath a wild rose-tree;
And, once upon a time, the violets clustered
So thick around it one could scarcely see;
And, once upon a time, a troop of children
Came dancing by upon the flowery ground;
And, once upon a time, the nest of fairies,
With shouts of joy and wonderment they found;
And, once upon a time, the fairies fluttered
On purple winglets, shimmering in the sun;
And, once upon a time, the nest forsaking,
They flew off thro' the violets, every one;
And, once upon a time, the children followed
With loud halloos along the meadow green;
And, once upon a time, the fairies vanished,
And never more could one of them be seen;
And, once upon a time, the children sought them
For many a day, but fruitless was their quest,
For, once upon a time, amid the violets,
They only found the fairies' empty nest.

Anything!

HOLLIE MCNISH

(for anyone else who still believes in fairies or elves or mermaids or wizards or...)

When I was eight years old
my friend Alex called me stupid
when I said I still believed
in things, like

fairies and wizards
and mermaids (with shell bikinis)
pixies and elves
and unicorns (with rainbow wee)

She said: *those things aren't really real!*
She said that I should grow up!
She said some others things as well
(but too rude for this poem)

Thing is, I *am* a grown up now
and I *still* believe in all these things
and if my friends laugh at me
this is what I sing:

Up above the world so high
A trillion twinkling little stars
And round each of those twinkling stars
A trillion planets spin like ours
A trillion planets we can't see
chilling out in outer space

Now think of all the things that live
here on earth, this one small place:

like butterflies (just hairier fairies aren't they, really?)
like whales as big as buses
Like shrimps whose hearts are in their heads
Like buzzing bees with two fat tummies
(one is just for making honey)

Like plants that gobble flies for tea
Like lily leaves as big as boats
Like spiders who pull threads
out their bums
to build their homes (sort of)

like tiger slugs with bright blue willies
like dinosaurs (well, in the past)
like the Bolson Pupfish fishes
who die if they don't fart

like deadly praying mantis bugs
who eat their boyfriends' heads! (Yuk)
Like dogs who sniff each other's bums
(why can't they just shake hands instead?)

If we have all this weird stuff HERE
on tiny little planet earth
and space is filled with trillions more
planet worlds that float and spin

then yes
I still believe
I shout

I believe
in
ANYTHING!

Readjustment

SUSAN COOLIDGE

After the earthquake shock or lightning dart
Comes a recoil of silence o'er the lands,
And then, with pulses hot and quivering hands,
Earth calls up courage to her mighty heart,
Plies every tender, compensating art,
Draws her green, flowery veil above the scar,
Fills the shrunk hollow, smooths the riven plain,
And with a century's tendance heals again
The seams and gashes which her fairness mar.
So we, when sudden woe like lightning sped,
Finds us and smites us in our guarded place,
After one brief, bewildered moment's space,
By the same heavenly instinct taught and led,
Adjust our lives to loss, make friends with pain,
Bind all our shattered hopes and bid them bloom again.

The Way Through the Woods

RUDYARD KIPLING

They shut the road through the woods
Seventy years ago.
Weather and rain have undone it again,
And now you would never know
There was once a road through the woods
Before they planted the trees.
It is underneath the coppice and heath,
And the thin anemones.
Only the keeper sees
That, where the ring-dove broods,
And the badgers roll at ease,
There was once a road through the woods.

Yet, if you enter the woods
Of a summer evening late,
When the night-air cools on the trout-ringed pools
Where the otter whistles his mate,
(They fear not men in the woods,
Because they see so few.)
You will hear the beat of a horse's feet,
And the swish of a skirt in the dew,
Steadily cantering through

The misty solitudes,
As though they perfectly knew
The old lost road through the woods.
But there is no road through the woods.

From Ode Number 7 from Book 4

HORACE

Translated from the Latin by Sabrina Mahfouz

Snow has scattered, returning green to the fields
and leaves to the trees:
Earth shifts with change,
and shrinking streams leave their banks with ease.

Frosts melt in the wind;
Summer crushes Spring,
Goodbye!
Autumn shares out its fruits;
soon Winter saunters over,
Hi!

Wood Between the Worlds

IONA LEE

In grows the gloaming,
and the forest and I have the new sky
all to ourselves.

I declare "Behold"
to no one.

Scotland
doused in Autumn.
The colours of a chewy bruise,
one that you would proudly present
to a friend.

I am stumbling
with the gait of the first girl.
Woodland, a warm towel
thrown round me.

Tripping over twisted roots,
skirts hitched, arms pricked
evergreen.

Withered branches bow
to wine-dark pools,
where midges flit
and carry fire.

I fantasise that if I jumped
I would be plunged into my past.

The wood between the worlds.

When I was wee
I would tie myself to bannisters
protesting a suggested walk.

A tiny suffragette
for the cause of not hiking.

I could be teased outside
with stories, though,
breadcrumbs placed along the way.

My memory is bosky,
but I can fathom from that phantom time
tales of Tam Lin and Ghillie Dhu.

Veiled within the forest,
a thousand lacing corridors,
the fairy hunt, forever running,
the pale Leshy, come to tempt me
to the woodland belly.
The Baba Yaga paddling air.

The damp smell of decay
hangs in the low-hanging sky
like a hammock, yet,
what a constant land!

From primeval Ask and Embla
to the elusive now, unbroken
mutability avowed.

The memories of my springtime days
are now almost as real as folklore.
The mind's eye shatters like the moon
is scattered between these broken pools.

Like a story will never be recited
twice the same.

Climbing

AMY LOWELL

High up in the apple tree climbing I go,
With the sky above me, the earth below.
Each branch is the step of a wonderful stair
Which leads to the town I see shining up there.

Climbing, climbing, higher and higher,
The branches blow and I see a spire,
The gleam of a turret, the glint of a dome,
All sparkling and bright, like white sea foam.

On and on, from bough to bough,
The leaves are thick, but I push my way through;
Before, I have always had to stop,
But to-day I am sure I shall reach the top.

Today to the end of the marvelous stair,
Where those glittering pinacles flash in the air!
Climbing, climbing, higher I go,
With the sky close above me, the earth far below.

The Oak

ALFRED, LORD TENNYSON

Live thy Life,
Young and old,
Like yon oak,
Bright in spring,
Living gold;

Summer-rich
Then; and then
Autumn-changed
Soberer-hued
Gold again.

All his leaves
Fall'n at length,
Look, he stands,
Trunk and bough
Naked strength.

Love is This Swamp

DEANNA RODGER

Love is the swamp we drove to today.
Along the reclaimed freeway,
one wrong turn late slow down
over the lip edge of the levee bowl.
True swamp emerged with its slicked edges
damning shading trees whose roots soak in Louisiana
  heat.
Love is this swamp.
Stick snakes three metres away
from our city neat feet and armadillos,
ancient and slow photographed crossing the soil road.
Pinned wood floats where solid ends.
Who knows who laid it, one wrong step
and I'll fall over the edge.
In this swamp, the water holds its green blanket so close
tricking me into seeing woods in the oak,
hearing Jurassic plants tip tap in the unexpected breeze.
Blocked pathway ahead, rain submerged my route.
No human could go on cleanly,
wading up to the heart through a swamp swollen
with deadly creatures.

Who knows how deep?
Too still to say.

The Statue

ELLA WHEELER WILCOX

A granite rock in the mountain side
Gazed on the world and was satisfied.
It watched the centuries come and go.
It welcomed the sunlight, yet loved the snow.
It grieved when the forest was forced to fall,
Yet joyed when steeples rose, white and tall,
In the valley below it, and thrilled to hear
The voice of the great town roaring near.

When the mountain stream from its idle play
Was caught by the mill wheel and borne away
And trained to labour, the grey rock mused
'Trees and verdure and stream are used
By Man the Master; but I remain
Friend of the mountain, and star, and plain,
Unchanged forever by God's decree,
While passing centuries bow to me.'

Then all unwarned, with a mighty shock
Out of the mountain was wrenched the rock.
Bruised and battered and broken in heart,

It was carried away to the common mart,
Wrecked and ruined in piece and pride.
'Oh, God is cruel,' the granite cried,
'Comrade of mountains, of stars the friend,
By all deserted, how sad my end.'

A dreaming sculptor in passing by
Gazed at the granite with thoughtful eye.
Then stirred with a purpose supremely grand
He bade his dream in the rock expand.
And lo! from the broken and shapeless mass
That grieved and doubted, it came to pass
That a glorious statue of priceless worth
And infinite beauty, adorned the earth.

The Bashful Earthquake

OLIVER HERFORD

The Earthquake rumbled
And mumbled And grumbled;
And then he bumped,
And everything tumbled—
Bumpyty-thump!
Thumpyty-bump!—
Houses and palaces all in a lump!
'Oh, what a crash!
Oh, what a smash!
How could I ever be so rash?'
The Earthquake cried.
'What under the sun
Have I gone and done?
I never before was so mortified!'
Then away he fled,
And groaned as he sped:
'This comes of not looking before I tread.'

Solitude

ARCHIBALD LAMPMAN

How still it is here in the woods. The trees
Stand motionless, as if they did not dare
To stir, lest it should break the spell. The air
Hangs quiet as spaces in a marble frieze.
Even this little brook, that runs at ease,
Whispering and gurgling in its knotted bed,
Seems but to deepen with its curling thread
Of sound the shadowy sun-pierced silences.

Sometimes a hawk screams or a woodpecker
Startles the stillness from its fixed mood
With his loud careless tap. Sometimes I hear
The dreamy white-throat from some far-off tree
Pipe slowly on the listening solitude
His five pure notes succeeding pensively.

Overheard on a Saltmarsh

HAROLD MONRO

Nymph, nymph, what are your beads?
Green glass, goblin. Why do you stare at them?
Give them me.
No.
Give them me. Give them me.
No.
Then I will howl all night in the reeds,
Lie in the mud and howl for them.
Goblin, why do you love them so?
They are better than stars or water,
Better than voices of winds that sing,
Better than any man's fair daughter,
Your green glass beads on a silver ring.
Hush, I stole them out of the moon.
Give me your beads, I want them.
No.
I will howl in the deep lagoon
For your green glass beads, I love them so.
Give them me. Give them.
No.

Peace and Pancakes

ADRIAN MITCHELL

the old world began
with a big bang
a big bang, a big bang

the new world begins
with a big song
a big song, a big song

it's got a strong beat
like your heartbeat
so use your two feet
to stomp out the beat

of a big song
of pancakes and peace
of a big song
everybody sing along

everybody loves pancakes
and everybody loves peace
you can find pancakes all around the world

north south west and east

dosas for breakfast in India
with spicy veg in the middle
Canadian maple syrup
on buckwheat cakes hot off the griddle
long live peace and pancakes!

the Greeks make pancakes with semolina
Russians make their blinis with yeast
red-hot quesadillas in Mexico City
yes pancakes turn any meal into a feast
long live peace and pancakes!

in Beijing they fill pancakes
with plum sauce and roast duck
every Shrove Tuesday in England
my pancake always gets stuck
    bad luck!
long live peace and pancakes!

the Koreans call their pancakes pa'chon
and cook'em with sesame seeds
the Romans serve cannelloni

pancakes are the banquet everyone needs
long live peace and pancakes!

South Africa's banana chapatis
Brittany's crêpes suzettes
every woman and man from Chile to Japan
they're eating all they can get

everybody loves pancakes
and everybody loves peace
you can find pancakes all around the world
north south west and east

long live the planet earth
long live the animals
long live the birds and fishes
long live the forests and oceans

long live the man
long live the woman
who use both courage and compassion
long live their children

long live peace
long live peace
long live peace and pancakes

Interim

LOLA RIDGE

The earth is motionless
And poised in space...
A great bird resting in its flight
Between the alleys of the stars.
It is the wind's hour off...
The wind has nestled down among the corn...
The two speak privately together,
Awaiting the whirr of wings.

Upon the Mountain's Distant Head

WILLIAM CULLEN BRYANT

Upon the mountain's distant head,
With trackless snows for ever white,
Where all is still, and cold, and dead,
Late shines the day's departing light.
But far below those icy rocks,
The vales, in summer bloom arrayed,
Woods full of birds, and fields of flocks,
Are dim with mist and dark with shade.
'Tis thus, from warm and kindly hearts,
And eyes where generous meanings burn,
Earliest the light of life departs,
But lingers with the cold and stern.

My Voice

PARTAW NADERI

Translated from the Dari by Sarah Maguire and Yama Yari

I come from a distant land
with a foreign knapsack on my back
with a silenced song on my lips

As I travelled down the river of my life
I saw my voice
(like Jonah)
swallowed by a whale

And my very life lived in my voice

My Heart's in the Highlands

ROBERT BURNS

My heart's in the Highlands, my heart is not here,
My heart's in the Highlands, a-chasing the deer;
Chasing the wild-deer, and following the roe,
My heart's in the Highlands, wherever I go.

Farewell to the Highlands, farewell to the North,
The birth-place of Valour, the country of Worth;
Wherever I wander, wherever I rove,
The hills of the Highlands for ever I love.

Farewell to the mountains, high-cover'd with snow,
Farewell to the straths and green vallies below;
Farewell to the forests and wild-hanging woods,
Farewell to the torrents and loud-pouring floods.

My heart's in the Highlands, my heart is not here,
My heart's in the Highlands, a-chasing the deer;
Chasing the wild-deer, and following the roe,
My heart's in the Highlands, wherever I go.

I Sing of Change

NIYI OSUNDARE

I sing
of the beauty of Athens
without its slaves

Of a world free
of kings and queens
and other remnants
of an arbitrary past

Of earth
with no
sharp north
or deep south
without blind curtains
or iron walls

of the end
of warlords and armouries
and prisons of hate and fear

Of deserts treeing
and fruiting
after quickening rains

Of the sun
radiating ignorance
and stars informing
nights of unknowing

I sing of a world reshaped

I Am / I Say (children's choral song)

SABRINA MAHFOUZ

I am the sea, I have something to say
I say
I don't want oil in my hair
Let me breathe coloured coral
Let me see my friend the sky.

I am the forest, I have something to say
I say
I don't want a fire in my throat
Let my leaves sing with birds
Let my roots roam with bugs.

I say
I say
I say

(Solo)

Close your eyes.
Think of a place that brings you peace
Makes you breathe in beauty

Can you see it?
Well I say
I say
I say

This place of peace
Is it trees or sky or ocean?
Tokens from a time when we knew
What we needed to survive.
Now our minds forget the scent of flowers
Our noses put to screens
Scream that what we need
Is money fame fame money
I say
I say
I say
Put your arms into arrows
Show the world you're on the way
To its heart.
Spark
Love spelt in leaves
Across skies fog forgets.
Imagine what we can do
Who we can be
If we all say

(Choir)

We are part of the heart of the world
Don't break it
Don't break it.
We don't have the power to make it turn
But we have the power to learn.
Don't shake it
like a fizzy drink,
Too much up and down
Too much throwing around
The pressure mounts
The insides explode
Goes all over your clothes
No!
We all have the power to learn
To turn it all around
Care for the earth from below the ground
To the rumbles of clouds

I say
I say

I may be small
But I want more than sweets
Give me a world that beats
With the beauty it was given
Before any of us were living.
We are part of the heart of the world
Don't break it.

Earth Song

A. F. HARROLD

Some of it is brown
and some of it is green.
Some of it is blue
and some is in between.

Some of it is local,
depending where you are.
Some of it is reachable
in a motorcar.

Some of it is dusty
and some of it is swampy.
Some of it is flat-ish
and some of it is lumpy.

Some of it's in darkness
and some of it's alight.
Some of it is frozen hard
and shining blinding white.

Some of it is poisoned
and some of it is dying.
Some of it is silent
and some of it is crying.

Some of it is going
and some of it is gone.
Some of it...

The Months

SARA COLERIDGE

January brings the snow,
makes our feet and fingers glow.

February brings the rain,
Thaws the frozen lake again.

March brings breezes loud and shrill,
stirs the dancing daffodil.

April brings the primrose sweet,
Scatters daisies at our feet.

May brings flocks of pretty lambs,
Skipping by their fleecy dams.

June brings tulips, lilies, roses,
Fills the children's hands with posies.

Hot July brings cooling showers,
Apricots and gillyflowers.

August brings the sheaves of corn,
Then the harvest home is borne.

Warm September brings the fruit,
Sportsmen then begin to shoot.

Fresh October brings the pheasants,
Then to gather nuts is pleasant.

Dull November brings the blast,
Then the leaves are whirling fast.

Chill December brings the sleet,
Blazing fire, and Christmas treat.

A Song of a Navajo Weaver

BERTRAND N. O. WALKER

For ages long, my people have been
    Dwellers in this land;
For ages viewed these mountains,
    Loved these mesas and these sands,
That stretch afar and glisten,
    Glimmering in the sun
As it lights the mighty canons
    Ere the weary day is done.
Shall I, a patient dweller in this
    Land of fair blue skies,
Tell something of their story while
    My shuttle swiftly flies?
As I weave I'll trace their journey,
    Devious, rough and wandering,
Ere they reached the silent region
    Where the night stars seem to sing.
When the myriads of them glitter
    Over peak and desert waste,
Crossing which the silent runner and
    The gaunt of co-yo-tees haste.
Shall I weave the zig-zag pathway

226

Whence the sacred fire was born;
And interweave the symbol of the God
　　Who brought the corn—
Of the Rain-god whose fierce anger
　　Was appeased by sacred meal,
And the trust that my brave people
　　In him evermore shall feel?
All this perhaps I might weave
　　As the woof goes to and fro,
Wafting as my shuttle passes,
　　Humble hopes, and joys and care,
Weaving closely, weaving slowly,
　　While I watch the pattern grow;
Showing something of my life:
　　To the Spirit God a prayer.
Grateful that he brought my people
　　To the land of silence vast
Taught them arts of peace and ended
　　All their wanderings of the past.
Deftly now I trace the figures,
　　This of joy and that of woe;
And I leave an open gate-way
　　For the Dau to come and go.

FIRE LEAPS

EXISTS THE FIRST IN LIGHT
AND THEN...

Bright Spark

MICHAELA MORGAN

Crouched cold in a cave,
huddled against the night.
What bright spark first made fire?
First made light?

That flash that made the world grow,
blazed spirits light, let faces glow,
to see each other.
Nod yes, shake no.

So, art is possible.
Stories can be shared.
Not now so lonely, silent, scared.

We can take flight.
Build a beacon.
Light.

Rainforest

JUDITH WRIGHT

The forest drips and glows with green.
the tree-frog croaks his far-off song.
His voice is stillness, moss and rain
drunk from the forest ages long.

We cannot understand that call
unless we move into his dream,
where all is one and one is all
and frog and python are the same.

We with our quick dividing eyes
measure, distinguish and are gone.
The forest burns, the tree-frog dies,
yet one is all and all are one.

Fire and Ice

ROBERT FROST

Some say the world will end in fire,
Some say in ice.
From what I've tasted of desire
I hold with those who favor fire.
But if it had to perish twice,
I think I know enough of hate
To say that for destruction ice
Is also great
And would suffice.

Fire in the Window

MARY MAPES DODGE

Fire in the window! flashes in the pane!
Fire on the roof-top! blazing weather-vane!
Turn about, weather-vane! put the fire out!
The sun's going down, sir, I haven't a doubt.

The Falling Star

SARA TEASDALE

I saw a star slide down the sky,
Blind the north as it went by,
Too burning and too quick to hold,
Too lovely to be bought or sold,
Good only to make wishes on
And then forever to be gone.

From Life

EMILY DICKINSON

You cannot put a fire out;
A thing that can ignite
Can go, itself, without a fan
Upon the slowest night.

You cannot fold a flood
And put it in a drawer,—
Because the winds would find it out,
And tell your cedar floor.

Ashes denote that fire was;
Respect the grayest pile
For the departed creature's sake
That hovered there awhile.

Fire exists the first in light,
And then consolidates,—
Only the chemist can disclose
Into what carbonates.

We the Fire Crowned Flares

HAFSAH ANEELA BASHIR

Fire leaps as steel and flint
Are quickly struck together,
Till bright sparks burn bright
To make the world a little better.

If I'm the flint and you're the steel
And we're sat around a campfire,
We'd crackle into circus hoops
To jump through till we're tired.

Our thoughts like white hot rockets
Would soar towards the sky
And if anyone tried to stop us
We'd become a flaming letter 'Y'.

We'd spread across the landscape
A wildfire of pure imagination,
Where the sun would only radiate
Beams of joyful exhilaration.

We'd hop scotch across volcanoes
Before the lava chased us down,

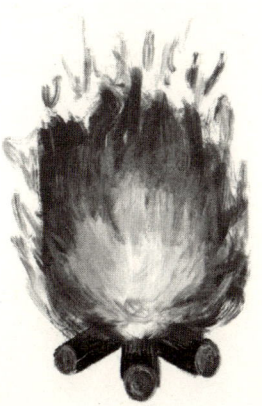

We'd comet through the oceans
Wearing our blazing fire-crowns.

Like flares of flashing fireflies
We'd light up every home,
We'd give ourselves like embers
To those who need it most.

Saying, fire leaps as steel and flint
Are quickly struck together,
Till bright sparks burn bright
To make the world a little better.

Paper

MONA ARSHI

We built each
other up with
paper;
origami
innards,
cardboard
skeletons
and   tissue
paper souls.
We slept on
shredded
paper,
had   our
younger
siblings   cut
and   colour
the moon,
the stars, the
sky.
Later   we
placed   paper

tigers in
playgrounds
constructed
giraffes with
concertina
necks
and
cultivated
gardens
rampant
with tiers of
crepe
flowers.
We turned
militant:
climbing
walls and
throwing
over paper
machier
grenades.
We bought
giant
machines
for

embossing
gigantic
cards
and   made
jagged edged
sky scrapers
which
stretched like
yawning
shard   arms
into the air.
Then we built
fire.
Before   long
paper   ash
snowflakes
filled   the
dead broken
back of the
sky.
Only   the
blind   birds
cried.

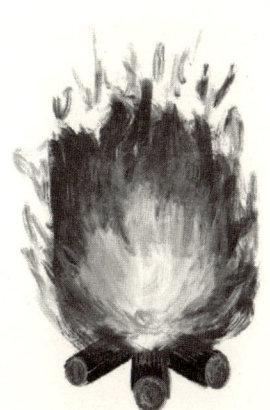

The Tyger

WILLIAM BLAKE

Tyger Tyger, burning bright,
In the forests of the night;
What immortal hand or eye,
Could frame thy fearful symmetry?

In what distant deeps or skies.
Burnt the fire of thine eyes?
On what wings dare he aspire?
What the hand, dare seize the fire?

And what shoulder, & what art,
Could twist the sinews of thy heart?
And when thy heart began to beat,
What dread hand? & what dread feet?

What the hammer? what the chain,
In what furnace was thy brain?
What the anvil? what dread grasp,
Dare its deadly terrors clasp!

When the stars threw down their spears
And water'd heaven with their tears:
Did he smile his work to see?
Did he who made the Lamb make thee?

Tyger Tyger burning bright,
In the forests of the night:
What immortal hand or eye,
Dare frame thy fearful symmetry?

Fire

DOROTHEA MACKELLAR

This life that we call our own
Is neither strong nor free;
A flame in the wind of death,
It trembles ceaselessly.

And this all we can do
To use our little light
Before, in the piercing wind,
It flickers into night:

To yield the heat of the flame,
To grudge not, but to give
Whatever we have of strength,
That one more flame may live.

My Light with Yours

EDGAR LEE MASTERS

I

When the sea has devoured the ships,
And the spires and the towers
Have gone back to the hills.
And all the cities
Are one with the plains again.
And the beauty of bronze,
And the strength of steel
Are blown over silent continents,
As the desert sand is blown—
My dust with yours forever.

II

When folly and wisdom are no more,
And fire is no more,
Because man is no more;
When the dead world slowly spinning
Drifts and falls through the void—
My light with yours
In the Light of Lights forever!

Thunder

ANNA AKHMATOVA

Translated from the Russian by A. S. Kline

There will be thunder then. Remember me.
Say – She asked for storms. The entire
world will turn the colour of crimson stone,
and your heart, as then, will turn to fire.

That day, in Moscow, a true prophecy,
when for the last time I say goodbye,
soaring to the heavens that I longed to see,
leaving my shadow here in the sky.

An Olive Fire

ROBERT WILLIAM SERVICE

An olive fire's a lovely thing;
Somehow it makes me think of Spring
As in my grate it over-spills
With dancing flames like daffodils.
They flirt and frolic, twist and twine,
The brassy fire-irons wink and shine…
Leap gold, you flamelets! Laugh and sing:
An olive fire's a lovely thing.

An olive fire's a household shrine:
A crusty loaf, a jug of wine,
An apple and a chunk of cheese –
Oh I could be content with these.
But if my curse of oil is there,
To fry a fresh-caught fish, I swear
I do not envy any king,
As sitting by my hearth I sing:
An olive fire's a lovely thing.

When old and worn, of life I tire,
I'll sit before an olive fire,

And watch the feather ash like snow
As softly as a rose heart glow;
The tawny roots will loose their hoard
Of sunbeams centuries have stored,
And flames like yellow chicken's cheep,
Till in my heart Peace is so deep:
With hands prayer-clasped I sleep... and sleep.

All in June

WILLIAM HENRY DAVIES

A week ago I had a fire
To warm my feet, my hands and face;
Cold winds, that never make a friend,
Crept in and out of every place.

Today the fields are rich in grass,
And buttercups in thousands grow;
I'll show the world where I have been—
With gold-dust seen on either shoe.

Till to my garden back I come,
Where bumble-bees for hours and hours
Sit on their soft, fat, velvet bums,
To wriggle out of hollow flowers.

First Fig

EDNA ST. VINCENT MILLAY

My candle burns at both ends;
It will not last the night;
But ah, my foes, and oh, my friends—
It gives a lovely light!

The Lights at Carney's Point

ALICE MOORE DUNBAR-NELSON

O white little lights at Carney's Point,
    You shine so clear o'er the Delaware;
When the moon rides high in the silver sky,
    Then you gleam, white gems on the Delaware.
Diamond circlet on a full white throat,
    You laugh your rays on a questioning boat;
Is it peace you dream in your flashing gleam,
    O'er the quiet flow of the Delaware?

And the lights grew dim at the water's brim,
    For the smoke of the mills shredded slow between;
And the smoke was red, as is new bloodshed,
    And the lights went lurid 'neath the livid screen.

O red little lights at Carney's Point,
    You glower so grim o'er the Delaware;
When the moon hides low sombrous clouds below,
    Then you glow like coals o'er the Delaware.
Blood red rubies on a throat of fire,
    You flash through the dusk of a funeral pyre;
And there hearth fires red whom you fear and dread
    O'er the turgid flow of the Delaware?

And the lights gleamed gold o'er the river cold,
　　For the murk of the furnace shed a copper veil;
And the veil was grim at the great cloud's brim,
　　And the lights went molten, now hot, now pale.

O gold little lights at Carney's Point,
　　You gleam so proud o'er the Delaware;
When the moon grows wan in the eastering dawn,
　　Then you sparkle gold points o'er the Delaware.
Aureate filagree on a Croesus' brow,
　　You hasten the dawn on a gray ship's prow.
Light you streams of gold in the grim ship's hold
　　O'er the sullen flow of the Delaware?

And the lights went gray in the ash of day,
　　For a quiet Aurora brought a halcyon balm;
And the sun laughed high in the infinite sky,
　　And the lights were forgot in the sweet, sane calm.

From **Home**

MARIETTA HOLLEY

A spirit is out to-night!
His steeds are the winds; oh, list,
How he madly sweeps o'er the clouds,
And scatters the driving mist.

We will let the curtains fall
Between us and the storm;
Wheel the sofa up to the hearth,
Where the fire is glowing warm.

The Fire of Drift-Wood

HENRY WADSWORTH LONGFELLOW

Devereux Farm, near Marblehead

We sat within the farm-house old,
    Whose windows, looking o'er the bay,
Gave to the sea-breeze damp and cold,
    An easy entrance, night and day.

Not far away we saw the port,
    The strange, old-fashioned, silent town,
The lighthouse, the dismantled fort,
    The wooden houses, quaint and brown.

We sat and talked until the night,
    Descending, filled the little room;
Our faces faded from the sight,
    Our voices only broke the gloom.

We spake of many a vanished scene,
    Of what we once had thought and said,
Of what had been, and might have been,
    And who was changed, and who was dead;

And all that fills the hearts of friends,
    When first they feel, with secret pain,
Their lives thenceforth have separate ends,
    And never can be one again;

The first slight swerving of the heart,
    That words are powerless to express,
And leave it still unsaid in part,
    Or say it in too great excess.

The very tones in which we spake
    Had something strange, I could but mark;
The leaves of memory seemed to make
    A mournful rustling in the dark.

Oft died the words upon our lips,
    As suddenly, from out the fire
Built of the wreck of stranded ships,
    The flames would leap and then expire.

And, as their splendor flashed and failed,
    We thought of wrecks upon the main,
Of ships dismasted, that were hailed
    And sent no answer back again.

The windows, rattling in their frames,
    The ocean, roaring up the beach,
The gusty blast, the bickering flames,
    All mingled vaguely in our speech;

Until they made themselves a part
    Of fancies floating through the brain,
The long-lost ventures of the heart,
    That send no answers back again.

O flames that glowed! O hearts that yearned!
    They were indeed too much akin,
The drift-wood fire without that burned,
    The thoughts that burned and glowed within.

Weather Proverb

ANONYMOUS

Red sky at night, shepherd's delight
Red sky in the morning, shepherd's warning

Midsummer

WILLIAM CULLEN BRYANT

A power is on the earth and in the air,
From which the vital spirit shrinks afraid,
And shelters him in nooks of deepest shade,
From the hot steam and from the fiery glare.
Look forth upon the earth – her thousand plants
Are smitten; even the dark sun-loving maize
Faints in the field beneath the torrid blaze;
The herd beside the shaded fountain pants;
For life is driven from all the landscape brown;
The bird hath sought his tree, the snake his den,
The trout floats dead in the hot stream, and men
Drop by the sunstroke in the populous town:
As if the Day of Fire had dawned, and sent
Its deadly breath into the firmament.

From The Aurora Australis

MARY HANNAY FOOTT

A radiance in the midnight sky
No white moon gave, nor yellow star;
We thought its red glow mounted high
Where fire and forest fought afar,

Half questioning if the township blazed,
Perchance, beyond the boundary hill;
Then, finding what it was, we gazed
And wondered till we shivered chill.

Flame Life

MAHD AL-AADIYYA

Translated from the Arabic by Abdullah Al-Udhari

I see people riding on shrieking horses,
steering clouds of sparkbelching fires
on their way to flame life out of you.

Across the Border

SOPHIE JEWETT

Where all the trees bear golden flowers,
    And all the birds are white;
Where fairy folk in dancing hours
    Burn stars for candlelight;

Where every wind and leaf can talk,
    But no man understand
Save one whose child-feet chanced to walk
    Green paths of fairyland;

I followed two swift silver wings;
    I stalked a roving song;
I startled shining, silent things;
    I wandered all day long.

But when it seemed the shadowy hours
    Whispered of soft-foot night,
I crept home to sweet common flowers,
    Brown birds, and candlelight.

Flint

CHRISTINA ROSSETTI

An emerald is as green as grass;
A ruby red as blood;
A sapphire shines as blue as heaven;
A flint lies in the mud.
A diamond is a brilliant stone,
To catch the world's desire;
An opal holds a fiery spark;
But a flint holds fire.

Autumn Fires

ROBERT LOUIS STEVENSON

In the other gardens
And all up the vale,
From the autumn bonfires
See the smoke trail!

Pleasant summer over
And all the summer flowers,
The red fire blazes,
The grey smoke towers.

Sing a song of seasons!
Something bright in all!
Flowers in the summer,
Fires in the fall!

From The Firemen's Ball

VACHEL LINDSAY

"Give the engines room,
Give the engines room."
Louder, faster
The little band-master
Whips up the fluting,
Hurries up the tooting.
He thinks that he stands,
The reins in his hands,
In the fire-chief's place
In the night alarm chase.
The cymbals whang,
The kettledrums bang: —
"Clear the street,
Clear the street,
Clear the street – Boom, boom.
In the evening gloom,
In the evening gloom,
Give the engines room,
Give the engines room.
Lest souls be trapped
In a terrible tomb."

The sparks and the pine-brands
Whirl on high
From the black and reeking alleys
To the wide red sky.
Hear the hot glass crashing,
Hear the stone steps hissing.
Coal black streams
Down the gutters pour.
There are cries for help
From a far fifth floor.
For a longer ladder
Hear the fire-chief call.
Listen to the music
Of the firemen's ball.
Listen to the music
Of the firemen's ball.
"'Tis the
NIGHT
Of doom,"
Say the ding-dong doom-bells.
"NIGHT
Of doom,"
Say the ding-dong doom-bells.

Faster, faster
The red flames come.
"Hum grum," say the engines,
"Hum grum grum."
"Buzz, buzz,"
Says the crowd.
"See, see,"
Calls the crowd.
And the high walls fall:—
Listen to the music
Of the firemen's ball
"'Tis the
NIGHT
Of doom,"
Say the ding-dong doom-bells.
NIGHT
Of doom,
Say the ding-dong doom-bells.
Whangaranga, whangaranga,
Whang, whang, whang,
Clang, clang, clangaranga,
Clang, clang, clang.
Clang—a—ranga—
Clang—a—ranga—

Clang,
Clang,
Clang.
Listen—to—the—music—
Of the firemen's ball—

II

"Many's the heart that's breaking
If we could read them all
After the ball is over."

(An old song)

Scornfully, gaily
The bandmaster sways,
Changing the strain
That the wild band plays.
With a red and royal intoxication,
A tangle of sounds
And a syncopation,
Sweeping and bending
From side to side,
Master of dreams,
With a peacock pride.

A lord of the delicate flowers of delight
He drives compunction
Back through the night.
Dreams he's a soldier
Plumed and spurred,
And valiant lads
Arise at his word,
Flaying the sober
Thoughts he hates,
Driving them back
From the dream-town gates.
How can the languorous
Dancers know
The red dreams come
When the good dreams go?
"'Tis the
NIGHT
Of love,"
Call the silver joy-bells,
"NIGHT
Of love,"
Call the silver joy-bells.
"Honey and wine,
Honey and wine.
Sing low, now, violins,

Sing, sing low,
Blow gently, wood-wind,
Mellow and slow.
Like midnight poppies
The sweethearts bloom.
Their eyes flash power,
Their lips are dumb.
Faster and faster
Their pulses come,
Though softer now
The drum-beats fall.
Honey and wine,
Honey and wine.
'Tis the firemen's ball,
'Tis the firemen's ball.

"I am slain,"
Cries true-love
There in the shadow.
"And I die,"
Cries true-love,
There laid low.
"When the fire-dreams come,
The wise dreams go."

BUT HIS CRY IS DROWNED
BY THE PROUD BAND-MASTER.

And now great gongs whang,
Sharper, faster,
And kettledrums rattle
And hide the shame
With a swish and a swirk
In dead love's name.
Red and crimson
And scarlet and rose
Magical poppies
The sweethearts bloom.
The scarlet stays
When the rose-flush goes,
And love lies low
In a marble tomb.
"'Tis the
NIGHT
Of doom,"
Call the ding-dong doom-bells.
"NIGHT
Of Doom,"
Call the ding-dong doom-bells.
Hark how the piccolos still make cheer.

'Tis a moonlight night in the spring of the year."
CLANGARANGA, CLANGARANGA,
CLANG… CLANG… CLANG.
CLANG… A… RANGA…
CLANG… A… RANGA…
CLANG… CLANG… CLANG…
LISTEN… TO… THE… MUSIC…
OF… THE… FIREMEN'S BALL…
LISTEN… TO… THE… MUSIC…
OF… THE… FIREMEN'S… BALL…

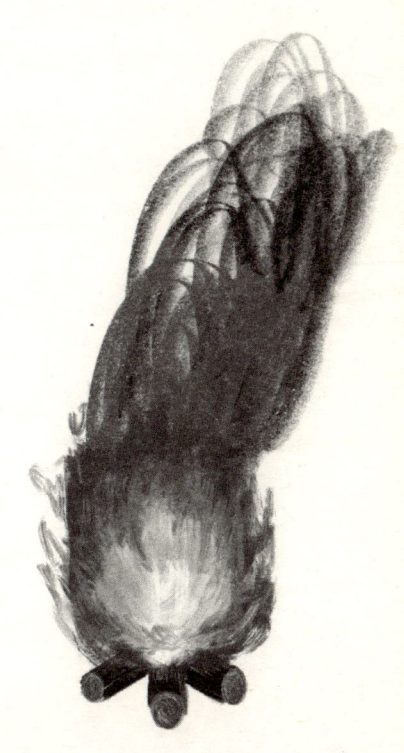

LIFE GROWS

YOU`LL BE A BUTTERFLY
BY AND BY...

Stream of Life

RABINDRANATH TAGORE

Translated from the Bengali by the poet

The same stream of life that runs through my veins night
    and day
runs through the world and dances in rhythmic
    measures.

It is the same life that shoots in joy through the dust of
    the earth
in numberless blades of grass
and breaks into tumultuous waves of leaves and flowers.

It is the same life that is rocked in the ocean-cradle of
    birth
and of death, in ebb and in flow.

I feel my limbs are made glorious by the touch of this
    world of life.
And my pride is from the life-throb of ages dancing in
    my blood this moment.

Flowering Tree Haiku

MATSUO BASHŌ

Translated from the Japanese by R. H. Blyth

From what flowering tree
I know not,
But ah, the fragrance!

From The Last Rose of Summer

THOMAS MOORE

'Tis the last rose of summer
   Left blooming alone;
All her lovely companions
   Are faded and gone;
No flower of her kindred,
   No rosebud is nigh,
To reflect back her blushes,
   To give sigh for sigh.

The Snail's Monologue

CHRISTIAN MORGENSTERN

Translated from the German by Max Knight

Shall I dwell in my shell?

Shall I not dwell in my shell?

Dwell in shell?

Rather not dwell?

Shall I not dwell?

Shall I dwell,

dwell in shell,

shall I shell,

shallIshellIshallIshellIshallI…?

If I Were a Rose

SABRINA MAHFOUZ

If I were a rose
I'd probably want redder petals
And a friend to rub the thorn from my side

If I were a rose
I'd probably want the rain wetter
And a personal patch of breeze to keep me dry

If I were a rose
I'd probably expect my stem to stay wilt-free
And for my life certainly not to end in a petrol station

A Toadstool Comes Up in a Night

CHRISTINA ROSSETTI

A toadstool comes up in a night, –
Learn the lesson, little folk: –
An oak grows on a hundred years,
But then it is an oak.

The Bluebell

ANNE BRONTË

A fine and subtle spirit dwells
In every little flower,
Each one its own sweet feeling breathes
With more or less of power.

There is a silent eloquence
In every wild bluebell
That fills my softened heart with bliss
That words could never tell.

Yet I recall not long ago
A bright and sunny day,
'Twas when I led a toilsome life
So many leagues away;

That day along a sunny road
All carelessly I strayed,
Between two banks where smiling flowers
Their varied hues displayed.

Before me rose a lofty hill,
Behind me lay the sea,
My heart was not so heavy then
As it was wont to be.

Less harassed than at other times
I saw the scene was fair,
And spoke and laughed to those around,
As if I knew no care.

But when I looked upon the bank
My wandering glances fell
Upon a little trembling flower,
A single sweet bluebell.

Whence came that rising in my throat,
That dimness in my eye?
Why did those burning drops distil,
Those bitter feelings rise?

O, that lone flower recalled to me
My happy childhood's hours
When bluebells seemed like fairy gifts
A prize among the flowers,

Those sunny days of merriment
When heart and soul were free,
And when I dwelt with kindred hearts
That loved and cared for me.

I had not then mid heartless crowds
To spend a thankless life
In seeking after others' weal
With anxious toil and strife.

'Sad wanderer, weep those blissful times
That never may return!'
The lovely floweret seemed to say,
And thus it made me mourn.

We Have a Little Garden

BEATRIX POTTER

We have a little garden,
A garden of our own,
And every day we water there
The seeds that we have sown.

We love our little garden,
And tend it with such care,
You will not find a faced leaf
Or blighted blossom there.

Greek Proverb

ANONYMOUS

A society grows great when old men plant trees whose shade they know they shall never sit in.

Tall Nettles

EDWARD THOMAS

Tall nettles cover up, as they have done
These many springs, the rusty harrow, the plough
Long worn out, and the roller made of stone:
Only the elm butt tops the nettles now.

This corner of the farmyard I like most:
As well as any bloom upon a flower
I like the dust on the nettles, never lost
Except to prove the sweetness of a shower.

Triolet

G. K. CHESTERTON

I wish I were a jelly fish
That cannot fall downstairs:
Of all the things I wish to wish
I wish I were a jelly fish
That hasn't any cares,
And doesn't even have to wish
'I wish I were a jelly fish
That cannot fall downstairs.'

O Dandelion

ANONYMOUS

"O dandelion, yellow as gold,
What do you do all day?"

*"I just wait here in the tall green grass
Till the children come to play."*

"O dandelion, yellow as gold,
What do you do all night?"

*"I wait and wait till the cool dews fall
And my hair grows long and white."*

"And what do you do when your hair is white
And the children come to play?"

*"They take me up in their dimpled hands
And blow my hair away!"*

Twinshoots

SAFIYYA BINT KHALID AL-BAHILIYYA
Translated from the Arabic by Abdullah Al-Udhari

1.

We were twinshoots sprouting beautifully on a tree.

2.

When our branches spread,
our shade stretched and our buds flushed,
time snapped my other shoot.

The Blackbird

HUMBERT WOLFE

In the far corner
close by the swings
every morning
a blackbird sings.

His bill's so yellow
his coat's so black
that he makes a fellow
whistle back.

Ann my daughter
thinks that he
sings for us two
especially.

Nature Poem

TALIA RANDALL

Right here on this bench a city idiot (me)
is stumped by the crocuses (croci?)

poking through the earth, like two fingers up
to the deep death of winter. Spring is stretching

her flabby limbs. Spring has her hair in a messy
bun, she's yawning and taking the kids to school

on her busy first day back. Do you ever feel like
it won't ever happen again? Spring in her early morning
   absent

mindedness will forget to return. When I was a
kid there was a nature reserve at the edge

of my estate. It was locked. All that bushy lushness
behind a padlock. We broke in, teasing

bolts from the bars and swinging them open.
We'd play there, pick berries, drink lemonade, like

those Enid Blyton kids except
authors wrote about us differently.

Not as individuals but as a litter, a swarm
a cluster, a mutation, a scraw, a knab, authors

grasping at the collective nouns.
They could have just given us names.

Right here on this bench I have acquired a new
language. One that is concerned with the correct

name for a thing. One that contemplates the crocus
and if it ever wanted to be called something else.

I Went to the Animal Fair

ANONYMOUS

I went to the Animal Fair,
The birds and the beasts were there.
The big baboon by the light of the moon,
Was combing his auburn hair.

The monkey fell out of the bunk,
And fell down the elephant's trunk.
The elephant sneezed and fell on his knees,
And what became of the monkey, monkey, monk?

How Pigeons Growl

DEAN ATTA

My niece believes all animals
Growl, that growl means animal.
She sees a dog and growls.
She sees a cat and growls.
She sees a pigeon and growls.
If I growl at her she will
Growl back. She crawls
After me. I crawl after her.
We play in ways I'd forgotten.
At times my fierceness startles her
Infant animal, she pauses
Pulls back her wide-eyed head,
Laugh-screams, picks up speed,
Giggling at animal me.

Winnebago Proverb

TRADITIONAL NATIVE AMERICAN

Of all the plants
that cover the earth
and lie like a fringe of hair
upon the body of our grandmother,
try to obtain knowledge
that you may be strengthened in life.

To a Squirrel at Kyle-Na-No

W. B. YEATS

Come play with me;
Why should you run
Through the shaking tree
As though I'd a gun
To strike you dead?
When all I would do
Is to scratch your head
And let you go.

The Microbe

HILAIRE BELLOC

The Microbe is so very small
You cannot make him out at all,
But many sanguine people hope
To see him through a microscope.
His jointed tongue that lies beneath
A hundred curious rows of teeth;
His seven tufted tails with lots
Of lovely pink and purple spots,
On each of which a pattern stands,
Composed of forty separate bands;
His eyebrows of a tender green;
All these have never yet been seen—
But Scientists, who ought to know,
Assure us that they must be so…
Oh! let us never, never doubt
What nobody is sure about!

With Birds You're Never Lonely

RAYMOND ANTROBUS

I can't hear the barista
over the coffee machine.

Spoons slam, steam rises.
I catch the eye of a man

sitting in the corner
of the cafe reading alone

about trees which is, incidentally,
all I can think about

since returning.
Last week I sat alone

on a stump, deep in Zelandia forest
with sun-syrupped Kauri trees

and brazen Tui birds with white tufts
and yellow and black beaks.

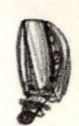

They landed by my feet, blaring so loudly
I had to turn off my hearing aids.

When all sound disappeared, I was tuned
into a silence that was not an absence.

As I switched sound on again,
silence collapsed.

The forest spat all the birds back,
and I was jealous—

the earthy Kauri trees, their endless
brown and green trunks of sturdiness.

I wondered what the trees
would say about us?

What books would they write
if they had to cut us down?

Later, stumbling from the forest I listened
to a young Maori woman.

She could tell which bird chirped,
a skill she learned from her grandfather

who said *with birds you're never lonely.*
In that moment I felt sorry

for any grey tree in London,
for the family they don't have,

the Gods they can't hold.

From Lines to a Shamrock – A Song of Exile

NORA PEMBROKE

A withered shamrock, yet to me 'tis fair
    As the sweet rose to other eyes might be,
  Because its leaves spread in my native air,
    And the same land gave birth to it and me.

They were as plentiful as drops of dew
    In our green meadows sprinkled everywhere,
  Heedless I wandered o'er them life was new,
    Now as a friend I greet thee shamrock fair.

A Scherzo (A Shy Person's Wishes)

DORA GREENWELL

With the wasp at the innermost heart of a peach,
On a sunny wall out of tip-toe reach,
With the trout in the darkest summer pool,
With the fern-seed clinging behind its cool
Smooth frond, in the chink of an aged tree,
In the woodbine's horn with the drunken bee,
With the mouse in its nest in a furrow old,
With the chrysalis wrapt in its gauzy fold;
With things that are hidden, and safe, and bold,
With things that are timid, and shy, and free,
Wishing to be;
With the nut in its shell, with the seed in its pod,
With the corn as it sprouts in the kindly clod,
Far down where the secret of beauty shows
In the bulb of the tulip, before it blows;
With things that are rooted, and firm, and deep,
Quiet to lie, and dreamless to sleep;
With things that are chainless, and tameless, and proud,
With the fire in the jagged thunder-cloud,
With the wind in its sleep, with the wind in its waking,
With the drops that go to the rainbow's making,

Wishing to be with the light leaves shaking,
Or stones on some desolate highway breaking;
Far up on the hills, where no foot surprises
The dew as it falls, or the dust as it rises;
To be couched with the beast in its torrid lair,
Or drifting on ice with the polar bear,
With the weaver at work at his quiet loom;
Anywhere, anywhere, out of this room!

How to Cut a Pomegranate

IMTIAZ DHARKER

'Never,' said my father,
'Never cut a pomegranate
through the heart. It will weep blood.
Treat it delicately, with respect.
Just slit the upper skin across four quarters.
This is a magic fruit,
so when you split it open, be prepared
for the jewels of the world to tumble out,
more precious than garnets,
more lustrous than rubies,
lit as if from inside.
Each jewel contains a living seed.
Separate one crystal.
Hold it up to catch the light.
Inside is a whole universe.
No common jewel can give you this.'
Afterwards, I tried to make necklaces
of pomegranate seeds.
The juice spurted out, bright crimson,
and stained my fingers, then my mouth.
I didn't mind. The juice tasted of gardens

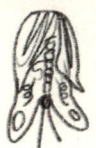

I had never seen, voluptuous
with myrtle, lemon, jasmine,
and alive with parrots' wings.
The pomegranate reminded me
that somewhere I had another home.

I Dunno

ANONYMOUS

I sometimes think I'd rather crow
And be a rooster than to roost
And be a crow. But I dunno.

A rooster he can roost also,
Which don't seem fair when crows can't crow
Which may help some. Still I dunno.

Crows should be glad of one thing though;
Nobody thinks of eating crows,
While roosters they are good enough
For anyone unless they are tough.

For there's a lot of tough old roosters though,
And anyway a crow can't crow,
So mebby roosters stand more show
It looks that way. But I dunno.

From **Antidote**

LUKA LESSON

In Ancient Greece
healers used to keep snakes,
they'd let them live beneath the beds of the sick
because they believed that snakes represented change,
renewal and healing.

Now,
in Greek the word for poison is
φαρμακι –
Farmaki
but the word for medicine
is φαρμακο
like pharmacy
because inside the poison
is where we find the antidote.

And they say –
'Live by the sword, die by the sword',
but the word sword
has the word 'word' in it
because our words can be the antidote…

So much so that we can retell history.

Sonnet 15: When I consider everything that grows

WILLIAM SHAKESPEARE

When I consider everything that grows
Holds in perfection but a little moment,
That this huge stage presenteth nought but shows
Whereon the stars in secret influence comment;
When I perceive that men as plants increase,
Cheered and check'd even by the selfsame sky,
Vaunt in their youthful sap, at height decrease,
And wear their brave state out of memory;
Then the conceit of this inconstant stay
Sets you most rich in youth before my sight,
Where wasteful Time debateth with Decay
To change your day of youth to sullied night;
And all in war with Time for love of you,
As he takes from you, I engraft you new.

A Soft White Feather Lying on the Grass

MONIZA ALVI

What does the feather say to the grass?
Well, nothing at all.
And yet there is a conversation –
filament to blade, blade to filament.
The feather gives the impression
of being complete in itself,
never part of something
never a fully-functioning part of a bird.
The blades clearly need each other
just as they require the feather
to bring them into brilliance.
Nothing is just white or green
or completely alone.
Is this true, or partly true?
The circumstance of the feather
touches the circumstance of the grass.
                               Both wait.
The grass is the more patient.

Rose and the Lily

ANONYMOUS

Rose dreamed she was a lily,
Lily dreamed she was a rose;
Robin dreamed he was a sparrow;
What the owl dreamed no one knows.

But they all woke up together
As happy as could be.
Said each: 'You're lovely, neighbour,
But I'm very glad I'm me.'

Don't Cry, Caterpillar

GRACE NICHOLS

Don't cry, Caterpillar
Caterpillar, don't cry
You'll be a butterfly – by and by.

Caterpillar, please
Don't worry about a thing

'But,' said Caterpillar,
'Will I still know myself – in wings?'

A Guinea Pig

ANONYMOUS

There was a little guinea pig,
Who being little, was not big;
He always walked upon his feet,
And never fasted when he eat.
When from a place he run away,
He never at the place did stay;
And while he run, as I am told,
He never stood still for young or old.
He often squeaked, and sometimes violent,
And when he squeaked he never was silent.
Though never instructed by a cat,
He knew a mouse was not a rat.
One day, as I am certified,
He took a whim, and fairly died;
And as I am told by men of sense,
He never has been living since.

Sunflower

MARJORIE LOTFI GILL

Her grandfather always said
that everything she'd need
was beneath the grey of its shell;
the signposts of winter would come
from its height, the strength
of its spine, how long it resisted
before nodding its head to wind.

When she left, she took nothing
but the seeds, their rattle in the tiny
tin better than money; no one else
would know the shade of soil
for planting, want flocks of birds
for friends. Now, she sleeps with them
under her pillow where they grow
into her dreams, stakes to lean against
on each crossing, and wakes
picking at yellow petals
tangled in her hair.

The Seedling

PAUL LAURENCE DUNBAR

As a quiet little seedling
Lay within its darksome bed,
To itself it fell a-talking,
And this is what it said:

"I am not so very robust,
But I'll do the best I can;"
And the seedling from that moment
Its work of life began.

So it pushed a little leaflet
Up into the light of day,
To examine the surroundings
And show the rest the way.

The leaflet liked the prospect,
So it called its brother, Stem;
Then two other leaflets heard it,
And quickly followed them.

To be sure, the haste and hurry
Made the seedling sweat and pant;
But almost before it knew it
It found itself a plant.

The sunshine poured upon it,
And the clouds they gave a shower;
And the little plant kept growing
Till it found itself a flower.

Little folks, be like the seedling,
Always do the best you can;
Every child must share life's labor
Just as well as every man.

And the sun and showers will help you
Through the lonesome, struggling hours,
Till you raise to light and beauty
Virtue's fair, unfading flowers.

Hurt No Living Thing

CHRISTINA ROSSETTI

Hurt no living thing:
Ladybird, nor butterfly,
Nor moth with dusty wing,
Nor cricket chirping cheerily,
Nor grasshopper so light of leap,
Nor dancing gnat, nor beetle fat,
Nor harmless worms that creep.

The Little Green Man Addresses a Leaf

JOHN AGARD

Spring's
new-sprung
earring

veined
no less

than human
flesh.

Shuffle Monster

DEAN ATTA

I was up way past my bedtime
Surfing the Internet one night
When a spider from the ceiling
Came down and gave me a fright

As it got closer it grew bigger
It was almost the size of my head
When it landed on my pillow
I used my iPad to squish it dead

But when I lifted my computer
The spider was nowhere to be found
I searched all over my bedroom
I looked up and down and all around

Then my iPad began to shuffle
It grew eight fat furry legs
And then right before my eyes
Began laying shiny silver eggs

What did those eggs become?
Is there one in your house or pocket
Is there one in your classroom
Plugged into an electrical socket?

While they are all connected
You should feel fear and dread
Because that is why the Internet
Is called the World Wide Web!

ICE CHILLS

DE LIP TURN BLUE, DE COLD,

ACHOO!

De

VALERIE BLOOM

De snow, de sleet, de lack o' heat,
De wishy-washy sunlight,
De lip turn blue, de cold, 'ACHOO!'
De runny nose, de frostbite,

De creakin' knee, de misery,
De joint dem all rheumatic,
De icy bed (de blanket dead),
De burs' pipe in de attic.

De window a-shake, de glass near break,
De wind dat cut like razor,
De wonderin' why you never buy
De window from dat double-glazer.

De heavy coat, zip to de throat,
De nose an' ears all pinky,
De weepin' sky, de clothes can't dry,
De day dem long an' inky.

De icy road, de heavy load,
De las' minute Christmas shoppin'
De cuss an' fret 'cause you feget
De ribbon an' de wrappin'.

De mud, de grime, de slush, de slime,
De place gloomy since November,
De sinkin' heart is jus de start, o'
De wintertime,
December.

From The Farewell Glacier

NICK DRAKE

When I was twelve
To win a bet
I walked across the thin ice of the frozen Severn
And never looked back.
Later, I resolved to walk
From Alaska to Svalbard
Across the sea ice
Via the Pole of Inaccessibility
And the North Pole.
My Inuit friends left a map
Pinned to the hut door
Marked with the places they thought I would die.
It was 3,800 miles;
We left in February,
Four men and forty dogs.
And in July we made camp
Because the ice was not drifting
In our favour.
When the sun returned
We continued through the next summer
To reach 90 degrees North.

I telegraphed the Queen.
Trying to stand on the pole
Was like trying to step
On the shadow of a bird
Circling overhead.
Two weeks later
A man took the first step on the Moon
And by the time we got home
We were forgotten.
You couldn't walk it now,
Even if you wanted to –
Why not?
Because the sea ice is melting,
And no one can walk on water.

From Snow-Bound

JOHN GREENLEAF WHITTIER

The sun that brief December day
Rose cheerless over hills of gray,
And, darkly circled, gave at noon
A sadder light than waning moon.

From Love's Labour's Lost

WILLIAM SHAKESPEARE

At Christmas I no more desire a rose
Than wish a snow in May's new-fangled mirth
But like of each thing that in season grows.

Wild Peaches

ELINOR WYLIE

1

When the world turns completely upside down
You say we'll emigrate to the Eastern Shore
Aboard a river-boat from Baltimore;
We'll live among wild peach trees, miles from town,
You'll wear a coonskin cap, and I a gown
Homespun, dyed butternut's dark gold color.
Lost, like your lotus-eating ancestor,
We'll swim in milk and honey till we drown.

The winter will be short, the summer long,
The autumn amber-hued, sunny and hot,
Tasting of cider and of scuppernong;
All seasons sweet, but autumn best of all.
The squirrels in their silver fur will fall
Like falling leaves, like fruit, before your shot.

2

The autumn frosts will lie upon the grass

Like bloom on grapes of purple-brown and gold.
The misted early mornings will be cold;
The little puddles will be roofed with glass.
The sun, which burns from copper into brass,
Melts these at noon, and makes the boys unfold
Their knitted mufflers; full as they can hold
Fat pockets dribble chestnuts as they pass.

Peaches grow wild, and pigs can live in clover;
A barrel of salted herrings lasts a year;
The spring begins before the winter's over.
By February you may find the skins
Of garter snakes and water moccasins
Dwindled and harsh, dead-white and cloudy-clear.

3

When April pours the colors of a shell
Upon the hills, when every little creek
Is shot with silver from the Chesapeake
In shoals new-minted by the ocean swell,
When strawberries go begging, and the sleek
Blue plums lie open to the blackbird's beak,
We shall live well – we shall live very well.

The months between the cherries and the peaches
Are brimming cornucopias which spill
Fruits red and purple, sombre-bloomed and black;
Then, down rich fields and frosty river beaches
We'll trample bright persimmons, while you kill
Bronze partridge, speckled quail, and canvasback.

4

Down to the Puritan marrow of my bones
There's something in this richness that I hate.
I love the look, austere, immaculate,
Of landscapes drawn in pearly monotones.
There's something in my very blood that owns
Bare hills, cold silver on a sky of slate,
A thread of water, churned to milky spate
Streaming through slanted pastures fenced with stones.

I love those skies, thin blue or snowy gray,
Those fields sparse-planted, rendering meagre sheaves;
That spring, briefer than apple-blossom's breath,
Summer, so much too beautiful to stay,
Swift autumn, like a bonfire of leaves,
And sleepy winter, like the sleep of death.

White Fields

JAMES STEPHENS

I
In the winter time we go
Walking in the fields of snow;

Where there is no grass at all;
Where the top of every wall,

Every fence, and every tree,
Is as white as white can be.

II
Pointing out the way we came –
Every one of them the same –

All across the fields there be
Prints in silver filigree;

And our mothers always know,
By the footprints in the snow,

Where it is the children go.

Weather Proverb

ANONYMOUS

Clear moon
Frost soon.

A Couplet

ITIMAD AR-RUMAIKIYYA
Translated from the Arabic by Sabrina Mahfouz

The wind rippled an armour's chainmail in the water,
What a shield it would make if it froze.

From London Snow

ROBERT BRIDGES

When men were all asleep the snow came flying,
In large white flakes falling on the city brown,
Stealthily and perpetually settling and loosely lying,
    Hushing the latest traffic of the drowsy town;
Deadening, muffling, stifling its murmurs failing;
Lazily and incessantly floating down and down:
    Silently sifting and veiling road, roof and railing;
Hiding difference, making unevenness even,
Into angles and crevices softly drifting and sailing.
    All night it fell, and when full inches seven
It lay in the depth of its uncompacted lightness,
The clouds blew off from a high and frosty heaven;
    And all woke earlier for the unaccustomed
     brightness
Of the winter dawning, the strange unheavenly glare:
The eye marvelled—marvelled at the dazzling whiteness;
    The ear hearkened to the stillness of the solemn air;
No sound of wheel rumbling nor of foot falling,
And the busy morning cries came thin and spare.

Dust of Snow

ROBERT FROST

The way a crow
Shook down on me
The dust of snow
From a hemlock tree

Has given my heart
A change of mood
And saved some part
Of a day I had rued.

February Twilight

SARA TEASDALE

I stood beside a hill
Smooth with new-laid snow,
A single star looked out
From the cold evening glow.

There was no other creature
That saw what I could see—
.I stood and watched the evening star
As long as it watched me.

A Snow Man

ANONYMOUS

Oh, the beautiful snow!
We're all in a glow—
Nell, Dolly, and Willie, and Dan;
For the primest of fun,
When all's said and done,
Is just making a big snow man.
Two stones for his eyes
Look quite owlishly wise,
A hard pinch of snow for his nose;
Then a mouth that's as big
As the snout of a pig,
And he'll want an old pipe, I suppose.
Then the snow man is done,
And to-morrow what fun
To make piles of snow cannon all day,
And to pelt him with balls
Till he totters and falls,
And a thaw comes and melts him away.

Christmas Roses

LIZZIE LAWSON

A bunch of Christmas Roses, dear,
   To greet my fairest child,
I plucked them in my garden where
   The drifting snow lay piled.

I cannot bring thee violets dear,
   Or cowslips growing wild,
Or daisy chain for thee to wear,
   For thee to wear, my child.

For all the grassy meadows near
   Are clad with snow, my child;
Through all the days of winter drear
   No ray of sun has smiled.

I plucked this bunch of verses, dear,
   From out my garden wild,
I plucked them in the winter drear
   For you, my fairest child,
Your wet and wintry hours to cheer,
   They're Christmas Roses, child.

Snowflakes

LEROY F. JACKSON

The snowflakes are falling
by ones and by twos;
There's snow on my jacket,
and snow on my shoes;
There's snow on the bushes,
and snow on the trees—
It's snowing on everything now,
if you please.

Snow in the Suburbs

THOMAS HARDY

Every branch big with it,
Bent every twig with it;
Every fork like a white web-foot;
Every street and pavement mute:
Some flakes have lost their way, and grope back upward
    when
Meeting those meandering down they turn and descend
    again.
The palings are glued together like a wall,
And there is no waft of wind with the fleecy fall.

A sparrow enters the tree,
Whereon immediately
A snow-lump thrice his own slight size
Descends on him and showers his head and eye
And overturns him,
And near inurns him,
And lights on a nether twig, when its brush
Starts off a volley of other lodging lumps with a rush.

The steps are a blanched slope,
Up which, with feeble hope,
A black cat comes, wide-eyed and thin;
And we take him in.

Describing Snow in the Aftermath

VANESSA KISUULE

The whole street would exhale
as if through a muzzle.
Faces squashed to greedy squints
we'd peer through the window,
greet the morning with a gasp.
Edible, treacherous, unrelenting
white, gobbling the ground, the sky, the
very thought of thought. Often,
our gloveless hands were shocked
back to life in scalding water.
Our mothers feared frostbite, but we
loved relearning our fingers. Nursed
back from numbness, they found
sport tracing rude words on windows.
We'd catch slippers to the backside.
Repentance briefly jogged our chests,
then left. The steady clockwork
of seasons and shame.

In the Garden

ANONYMOUS

Greedy little sparrow,
Great big crow,
Saucy little tom-tits
All in a row.

Are you very hungry,
No place to go?
Come and eat my breadcrumbs,
In the snow.

On the Hard Crest

ANNA AKHMATOVA

Translated from the Russian by A.S. Kline

On the hard crest of a snowdrift,
To your white mysterious house,
So silent, in the silence,
Both through gentle silence go.
And the sweetest song sung to me,
Sweeter than any song ever sung,
The swaying of lightly-touched branches,
The slight ringing sound of your spurs.

Up in the Morning Early

ROBERT BURNS

Cauld blaws the wind frae east to west,
The drift is driving sairly;
Sae loud and shrill's I hear the blast,
I'm sure it's winter fairly.

Up in the morning's no for me,
Up in the morning early;
When a' the hills are cover'd wi' snaw,
I'm sure it's winter fairly.

The birds sit chittering in the thorn,
A' day they fare but sparely;
And lang's the night frae e'en to morn,
I'm sure it's winter fairly.

Up in the morning's no for me,
Up in the morning early;
When a' the hills are cover'd wi' snaw,
I'm sure it's winter fairly.

From With Solid Drops

IBN KHAFAJAH

Translated from the Arabic by Sabrina Mahfouz

With solid drops the hail that showers down
has often laid around the neck of Mother Earth.
The frozen water fires the fields with small stones
and the land is covered by unwelcome melting.
The earth laughs, shows off its necklaces of stars,
but once they are unstrung, gone,
the sky is moody, furious.

Stopping by Woods on a Snowy Evening

ROBERT FROST

Whose woods these are I think I know.
His house is in the village, though;
He will not see me stopping here
To watch his woods fill up with snow.

My little horse must think it's queer
To stop without a farmhouse near
Between the woods and frozen lake
The darkest evening of the year.

He gives his harness bells a shake
To ask if there's some mistake.
The only other sound's the sweep
Of easy wind and downy flake.

The woods are lovely, dark, and deep,
But I have promises to keep,
And miles to go before I sleep,
And miles to go before I sleep.

From Snow

ELIZA COOK

A cheer for the snow – the drifting snow!
Smoother and purer than beauty's brow!
The creature of thought scarce likes to tread
On the delicate carpet so richly spread.
With feathery wreaths the forest is bound,
And the hills are with glittering diadems crown'd;
'Tis the fairest scene we can have below.
Sing, welcome, then, to the drifting snow!

The Last Snow Leopard

SABRINA MAHFOUZ

A track, a print, a paw.
Trailing, tripping for a flake of a glimpse
of blue eyes, grey fur against black stone;
We'll stay until we find her.

Search the ice to catch a breathless sight,
rocks crumbling underneath calloused feet,
mouths moving frozen whispers;
Don't scare her away.

But she's far from being scared.
It's her landscape,
it's us who lay caught:
unprepared, unaware, unknowing.

A slashed-throat goat by morning
blood-drips the directions no map could.
Electric beeps meaningless
to a legend who has roamed these rocks for centuries.

We log the location of her den,
coordinates to keep her safe, supposedly.
Then –
three cubs tremble bravely out into the snow,
rolling over each other like a tombola –
we did not find the last snow leopard after all.

Jack Frost

CELIA THAXTER

Rustily creak the crickets: Jack Frost came down last night,
He slid to earth on a starbeam, keen and sparkling bright;
He sought in the grass for the crickets with delicate icy
    spear,
So sharp and fine and fatal, and he stabbed them far
    and near.
Only a few stout fellows, thawed by the morning sun,
Chirrup a mournful echo of by-gone frolic and fun.
But yesterday such a rippling chorus ran all over the land,
Over the hills and the valleys, down to the gray sea-sand,
Millions of merry harlequins, skipping and dancing
    in glee,
Cricket and locust and grasshopper, happy as happy
    could be:
Scooping rich caves in ripe apples, and feeding on honey
    and spice,
Drunk with the mellow sunshine, nor dreaming of spears
    of ice!

Snow Pie Time

SALENA GODDEN

Professor Snow has hair of white
His beard is soft as snow
He wants to invent a time machine
To make time on earth go slow

Busy in his laboratory
He works throughout the night
Stirring time with ice and spice
And shaking them just right

He captured the tick and the tock
Whisked snow with milk and heat
He took the past, the first and last
And made the two ends meet

He took apart his cuckoo clock
To seek the source of time
He ate the cuckoo for his tea
Fried in treacle, lime and thyme

He believed that golden time
Should drift out of the sky
But all it did was snow and snow
and he did not know why

Out walking in the snowy woods
The snow fell fast and thick
He wished he could slow down time
He wished it was not such a sneaky trick

The Professor sighed, tipped back his head
A snowflake landed on his tongue
It tasted as sweet as olden times
And took him back to being young

All the icy rivers gurgled and giggled
With life before and stories told
Snowflakes are like free ice cream
And time is always gold

Professor Snow laughed and laughed
Eating fat snowballs in his fists
He sucked icicles for pudding
Death is long if life is missed

The taste of snow will take you back
When you're young and when you're old
Snow pies are forever wonderful
Your life is precious and time is gold.

The Skaters

JOHN GOULD FLETCHER

Black swallows swooping or gliding
In a flurry of entangled loops and curves;
The skaters skim over the frozen river.
And the grinding click of their skates as they impinge
    upon the surface,
Is like the brushing together of thin wing-tips of silver.

The Quiet Snow

RAYMOND KNISTER

The quiet snow
Will splotch
Each in the row of cedars
With a fine
And patient hand;
Numb the harshness,
Tangle of that swamp.
It does not say, The sun
Does these things another way.

Even on hats of walkers,
The air of noise
And street-car ledges
It does not know
There should be hurry.

Something Told the Wild Geese

RACHEL FIELD

Something told the wild geese
It was time to go.
Though the fields lay golden
Something whispered, – 'Snow.'
Leaves were green and stirring,
Berries, luster-glossed,
But beneath warm feathers
Something cautioned, – 'Frost.'
All the sagging orchards
Steamed with amber spice,
But each wild breast stiffened
At remembered ice.
Something told the wild geese
It was time to fly,—
Summer sun was on their wings,
Winter in their cry.

Winter-Lull

D. H. LAWRENCE

Because of the silent snow, we are all hushed
       Into awe.
No sound of guns, nor overhead no rushed
       Vibration to draw
Our attention out of the void wherein we are crushed.
A crow floats past on level wings
       Noiselessly.
Uninterrupted silence swings
       Invisibly, inaudibly
To and fro in our misgivings.
We do not look at each other, we hide
       Our daunted eyes.
White earth, and ruins, ourselves, and nothing beside.
       It all belies
Our existence; we wait, and are still denied.
We are folded together, men and the snowy ground
       Into nullity.
There is silence, only the silence, never a sound
       Nor a verity
To assist us; disastrously silence-bound!

A Windflower

LIZETTE WOODWORTH REESE

The wind stooped down and wrote a sweet, small word,
But the snow fell, and all the writing blurred:
Now, the snow gone, we read it as we pass,—
The wind's word in the grass.

The Elephant is Walking on the River Thames

IMTIAZ DHARKER

The whole city has come out to see the river
frozen over, solid enough to light a blazing fire
and spit-roast a whole ox, a suckling pig,
sparks in the air, fat hissing on silver,

mutton pies sizzling. Red-nosed boys
slide past St Paul's, horses pull sledges of coal
under the bridge, and then this:
an elephant steps carefully on to the ice.

The known world

cracks. Reality lumbers over the edge.
Hawkers freeze, pour ale into mid-air
as the creature sails by, more
graceful than any stilt-walker or skater.

Later they will recall it
like something suspended in time,

like first love at the last frost fair.
They will say, *That was the day. I was there.*

Snow Fox

LIZ BROWNLEE

In the Arctic summer
the cloud-grey fox
listens for prey
in the low shrubs and rocks

grizzled and still
as the permafrost ground
his senses vivid
with scent and sound

when lemmings are hidden
under the snow
the wild geese are flown
and biting winds blow

a horizon-less white
shrouds the Arctic fox
in clouds of snow fur
from tail-tip to socks

he haunts frozen sea
as thin as the air
hoping for scraps
missed by polar bear

or curls in his tail
from the star-cold white
chewing on hunger
through long Arctic night

and waits for spring sun
and pale Arctic day
to melt tundra snow
and his white coat away

From **Frost at Midnight**

SAMUEL TAYLOR COLERIDGE

The Frost performs its secret ministry,
Unhelped by any wind. The owlet's cry
Came loud – and hark, again! loud as before.
The inmates of my cottage, all at rest,
Have left me to that solitude, which suits
Abstruser musings: save that at my side
My cradled infant slumbers peacefully.
'Tis calm indeed! so calm, that it disturbs
And vexes meditation with its strange
And extreme silentness. Sea, hill, and wood,
This populous village! Sea, and hill, and wood,
With all the numberless goings-on of life,
Inaudible as dreams!

The Thaw

HENRY DAVID THOREAU

I saw the civil sun drying earth's tears –
Her tears of joy that only faster flowed,

Fain would I stretch me by the highway side,
To thaw and trickle with the melting snow,
That mingled soul and body with the tide,
I too may through the pores of nature flow.

But I alas nor tinkle can nor fume,
One jot to forward the great work of Time,
'Tis mine to hearken while these ply the loom,
So shall my silence with their music chime.

Snow

EDWARD THOMAS

In the gloom of whiteness,
In the great silence of snow,
A child was sighing
And bitterly saying: 'Oh,
They have killed a white bird up there on her nest.
The down is fluttering from her breast!'
And still it fell through that dusky brightness
On the child crying for the bird of the snow.

MOON RISES

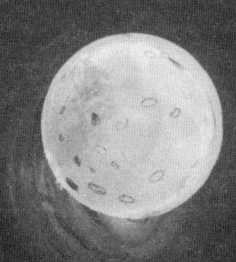

WITH SILENT DELIGHT SITS
AND SMILES ON THE NIGHT...

The Moon Haiku

NIKYU

Translated from the Japanese by R. H. Blyth

Between the moon coming out
And the sun going in —
The red dragonflies.

Dancing Disk in the Sky

HIBAQ OSMAN

If you asked what The Moon is
people would tell you
in their proudest voices:

The Moon is a circle in the sky
waiting for your greeting
you should say hello
in any of the languages you know
or maybe say them all
just in case!

The Moon is a reflection in the water
that jiggles with the wind
It is a silver plate dancing with you
by the river bank

It has many friends
who speak to it at night
and you, with your small voice,
no need to worry
The Moon is a very good listener!

Look up and see
if you peek behind your curtains
The Moon will dance for us
so nobody feels lonely.

Scottish Proverb

ANONYMOUS

The day has eyes.
The night has ears.

Five Little Owls

ANONYMOUS

Five little owls in an old elm tree,
Fluffy and puffy as owls could be,
Blinking and winking with big round eyes
At the big round moon that hung in the skies:
As I passed beneath I could hear one say,
"There'll be mouse for supper, there will, today!"
Then all of them hooted "Tu-whit tu-whoo!
Yes, mouse for supper, hoo hoo! Hoo hoo!"

From Drifting Flowers of the Sea

SADAKICHI HARTMANN

Across the dunes, in the waning light,
The rising moon pours her amber rays,
Through the slumbrous air of the dim, brown night
The pungent smell of the seaweed strays—
From vast and trackless spaces
Where wind and water meet,
White flowers, that rise from the sleepless deep,
Come drifting to my feet.
They flutter the shore in a drowsy tune,
Unfurl their bloom to the lightlorn sky,
Allow a caress to the rising moon,
Then fall to slumber, and fade, and die.

From **Summer in London**

HELEN LEAH REED

Oh, the noise of Piccadilly – its rumble and its roar!
A tide of life's broad ocean surging toward the shore.
Who once has listened, ever can hear its long refrain
With haunting echo drowning or dirge or flaunting
    strain.
Who heeds it, in his vision may see a world-throng
    pass –
And over there the Green Park with laughing lad and
    lass;
While weary men and women and careless youth go by,
Where windows glow and glitter, and in the evening sky
A crescent moon is watching the laughing lass and lad.
The long, warm London twilight! Happy they are,
    though sad.
With kiss and tear they are parting. 'Tis late – the rush
    and roar –
The life of Piccadilly is waning – is no more.

Seal Lullaby

RUDYARD KIPLING

Oh! hush thee, my baby, the night is behind us,
And black are the waters that sparkled so green.
The moon, o'er the combers, looks downward to find us
At rest in the hollows that rustle between.
Where billow meets billow, there soft be thy pillow;
Ah, weary wee flipperling, curl at thy ease!
The storm shall not wake thee, nor shark overtake thee,
Asleep in the arms of the slow-swinging seas.

Night

WILLIAM BLAKE

The sun descending in the west,
The evening star does shine;
The birds are silent in their nest,
And I must seek for mine.
The moon, like a flower,
In heaven's high bower,
With silent delight
Sits and smiles on the night.

Farewell, green fields and happy groves,
Where flocks have took delight.
Where lambs have nibbled, silent moves
The feet of angels bright;
Unseen they pour blessing,
And joy without ceasing,
On each bud and blossom,
And each sleeping bosom.

They look in every thoughtless nest,
Where birds are covered warm;

They visit caves of every beast,
To keep them all from harm.
If they see any weeping
That should have been sleeping,
They pour sleep on their head,
And sit down by their bed.

When wolves and tigers howl for prey,
They pitying stand and weep;
Seeking to drive their thirst away,
And keep them from the sheep.
But if they rush dreadful,
The angels, most heedful,
Receive each mild spirit,
New worlds to inherit.

And there the lion's ruddy eyes
Shall flow with tears of gold,
And pitying the tender cries,
And walking round the fold,
Saying, 'Wrath, by His meekness,
And, by His health, sickness
Is driven away
From our immortal day.

'And now beside thee, bleating lamb,
I can lie down and sleep;
Or think on Him who bore thy name,
Graze after thee and weep.
For, washed in life's river,
My bright mane for ever
Shall shine like the gold
As I guard o'er the fold.'

November Night

ADELAIDE CRAPSEY

Listen...
With faint dry sound,
Like steps of passing ghosts,
The leaves, frost-crisp'd, break from the trees
And fall.

From A Midsummer Night's Dream

WILLIAM SHAKESPEARE

You spotted snakes with double tongue,
Thorny hedgehogs, be not seen;
Newts and blindworms, do no wrong,
Come not near our fairy Queen.
Philomele, with melody
Sing in our sweet lullaby;
Lulla, lulla, lullaby, lulla, lulla, lullaby:
Never harm
Nor spell nor charm,
Come our lovely lady nigh;
So, good night, with lullaby.
Weaving spiders, come not here;
Hence, you long-legged spinners, hence!
Beetles black, approach not near;
Worm nor snail, do no offence.
Philomele, with melody
Sing in our sweet lullaby;
Lulla, lulla, lullaby, lulla, lulla, lullaby:
Never harm
Nor spell nor charm,
Come our lovely lady nigh;
So, good night, with lullaby.

Weather Proverb

ANONYMOUS

Cold is the night
When the stars shine bright.

Weather Proverb

ANONYMOUS

A ring around the moon...
Rain real soon.

Spellbound

EMILY BRONTË

The night is darkening round me,
The wild winds coldly blow;
But a tyrant spell has bound me
And I cannot, cannot go.
The giant trees are bending
Their bare boughs weighed with snow.
And the storm is fast descending,
And yet I cannot go.
Clouds beyond clouds above me,
Wastes beyond wastes below;
But nothing drear can move me;
I will not, cannot go.

Beehive

JEAN TOOMER

Within this black hive to-night
There swarm a million bees;
Bees passing in and out the moon,
Bees escaping out the moon,
Bees returning through the moon,
Silver bees intently buzzing,
Silver honey dripping from the swarm of bees
Earth is a waxen cell of the world comb,
And I, a drone,
Lying on my back,
Lipping honey,
Getting drunk with that silver honey,
Wish that I might fly out past the moon
And curl forever in some far-off farmyard flower.

What If the Moon Is a Refugee?

SALENA GODDEN

a blind old lady with silver eyes
all milky-white her face
her begging bowl is shining stars
and deep as outer space
her begging bowl is shooting stars
and deep as outer space
that blind old lady is the silver moon
and all milky-white her face

Bedtime

THOMAS HOOD

The evening is coming,
The sun sinks to rest;
The rooks are all flying
Straight home to the nest.
"Caw!" says the rook, as he flies overhead;
"It's time little people were going to bed!"

The flowers are closing;
The daisy's asleep;
The primrose is buried
In slumber so deep.
Shut up for the night is the pimpernel red;
It's time little people were going to bed!

The butterfly, drowsy,
Has folded its wing;
The bees are returning,
No more the birds sing.
Their labour is over, their nestlings are fed;
It's time little people were going to bed!

Here comes the pony,
His work all done;
Down through the meadow
He takes a good run;
Up goes his heels and down goes his head;
It's time little people were going to bed!

Good night, little people,
Good night and good night;
Sweet dreams to your eyelids
Till dawning of light;
The evening has come, there's no more to be said,
It's time little people were going to bed!

The Fog

F. R. MCCREARY

Slowly the fog,
Hunched-shouldered with a grey face,
Arms wide, advances
Finger-tips touching the way
Past dark houses
And dark gardens of roses.
Up the short street from the harbor,
Slowly the fog,
Seeking, seeking;
Arms wide, shoulders hunched,
Searching, searching
Out through the streets to the fields,
Slowly the fog –
A blind man hunting the moon.

If You Were an Owl

MARY MAPES DODGE

If you were an owl,
And I were an owl,
And this were a tree,
And the moon came out,
I know what we'd do.
We would stand, we two,
On a bough of the tree;
You'd wink at me,
And I'd wink at you;
That's what we'd do,
Beyond a doubt.

I'd give you a rose –
For your lovely nose,
And you'd look at me
Without turning about.
I know what we'd do
(That is, I and you);
Why, you'd sing to me,
And I'd sing to you;
That's what we'd do,
When the moon came out.

The Wind and the Moon

GEORGE MACDONALD

Said the Wind to the Moon, "I will blow you out;
You stare
In the air
Like a ghost in a chair,
Always looking what I am about –
I hate to be watched; I'll blow you out."

The Wind blew hard, and out went the Moon.
So, deep
On a heap
Of clouds to sleep,
Down lay the Wind, and slumbered soon,
Muttering low, "I've done for that Moon."

He turned in his bed; she was there again!
On high
In the sky,
With her one ghost eye,
The Moon shone white and alive and plain.
Said the Wind, "I will blow you out again."

The Wind blew hard, and the Moon grew dim.
"With my sledge,
And my wedge,
I have knocked off her edge!
If only I blow right fierce and grim,
The creature will soon be dimmer than dim."

He blew and he blew, and she thinned to a thread.
"One puff
More's enough
To blow her to snuff!
One good puff more where the last was bred,
And glimmer, glimmer, glum will go the thread."

He blew a great blast, and the thread was gone.
In the air
Nowhere
Was a moonbeam bare;
Far off and harmless the shy stars shone –
Sure and certain the Moon was gone!

The Wind he took to his revels once more;
On down,
In town,
Like a merry-mad clown,

He leaped and halloed with whistle and roar –
"What's that?" The glimmering thread once more!

He flew in a rage – he danced and blew;
But in vain
Was the pain
Of his bursting brain;
For still the broader the Moon-scrap grew,
The broader he swelled his big cheeks and blew.

Slowly she grew – till she filled the night,
And shone
On her throne
In the sky alone,
A matchless, wonderful silvery light,
Radiant and lovely, the queen of the night.

Said the Wind: "What a marvel of power am I!
With my breath,
Good faith!
I blew her to death –
First blew her away right out of the sky –
Then blew her in; what strength have I!

But the Moon she knew nothing about the affair;
For high
In the sky,
With her one white eye,
Motionless, miles above the air,
She had never heard the great Wind blare.

Birch Trees

JOHN RICHARD MORELAND

The night is white,
The moon is high,
The birch trees lean
Against the sky.

The cruel winds
Have blown away
Each little leaf
Of silver gray.

O lonely trees
As white as wool…
That moonlight makes
So beautiful.

I Had a Boat

MARY COLERIDGE

I had a boat, and the boat had wings;
   And I did dream that we went a flying
Over the heads of queens and kings,
   Over the souls of dead and dying,
Up among the stars and the great white rings,
   And where the Moon on her back is lying.

From The Starlight Night

GERARD MANLEY HOPKINS

Look at the stars! look, look up at the skies!
   O look at all the fire-folk sitting in the air!
   The bright boroughs, the circle-citadels there!
Down in dim woods the diamond delves! the
   elves'-eyes!
The grey lawns cold where gold, where quickgold lies!

The Crescent Moon

AMY LOWELL

Slipping softly through the sky
Little horned, happy moon,
Can you hear me up so high?
Will you come down soon?

On my nursery window-sill
Will you stay your steady flight?
And then float away with me
Through the summer night?

Brushing over tops of trees,
Playing hide and seek with stars,
Peeping up through shiny clouds
At Jupiter or Mars.

I shall fill my lap with roses
Gathered in the milky way,
All to carry home to mother.
Oh! what will she say!

Little rocking, sailing moon,
Do you hear me shout – Ahoy!
Just a little nearer, moon,
To please a little boy.

The Algonquin Calendar of Changing Moons

CHERYL MOSKOWITZ

Dark nights growing

Wolf Moon
Snow Moon
Worm Moon

Nobody likes me

Buds start showing

Pink Moon
Flower Moon
Strawberry Moon

Served with cream and a silver spoon

Warm sun glowing

Buck Moon
Sturgeon Moon
Harvest Moon

Last one home's a pumpkin!

Leaves are blowing

Hunter's Moon
Beaver Moon
Cold Moon

When the year ends will you still be my friend?

Love bestowing

My Moon
Your Moon
Blue Moon

Round the earth and back again

Summer Stars

CARL SANDBURG

Bend low again, night of summer stars.
So near you are, sky of summer stars,
So near, a long arm man can pick off stars,
Pick off what he wants in the sky bowl,
So near you are, summer stars,
So near, strumming, strumming,
So lazy and hum-strumming.

From The Bat

JAMES WHITCOMB RILEY

Thou dread, uncanny thing,
With fuzzy breast and leathern wing,
In mad, zigzagging flight,
Notching the dusk, and buffeting
The black cheeks of the night,
With grim delight!

Night Comes

BEATRICE SCHENK DE REGNIERS

Night comes
leaking
out of the sky.
Stars come
peeking.
Moon comes
sneaking,
silvery-sly.
Who is
shaking
shivery-
quaking?
Who is afraid
of the night?
Not I.

The Moon

ROBERT LOUIS STEVENSON

The moon has a face like the clock in the hall;
She shines on thieves on the garden wall,
On streets and fields and harbour quays,
And birdies asleep in the forks of the trees.

The squalling cat and the squeaking mouse,
The howling dog by the door of the house,
The bat that lies in bed at noon,
All love to be out by the light of the moon.

But all of the things that belong to the day
Cuddle to sleep to be out of her way;
And flowers and children close their eyes
Till up in the morning the sun shall arise.

From On the Road to the Sea

CHARLOTTE MEW

Oh! let it rest;
I will not stare into the early world beyond the opening
   eyes,
      Or vex or scare what I love best.
      But I want your life before mine bleeds
         away—
            Here – not in heavenly hereafters – soon,—
            I want your smile this very afternoon,
         (The last of all my vices, pleasant people used
            to say,
               I wanted and I sometimes got – the Moon!)

      You know, at dusk, the last bird's cry,
   And round the house the flap of the bat's low flight,
      Trees that go black against the sky
      And then – how soon the night!

Cushlamochree

LUCY COATS

Cushlamochree, O Cushlamochree
Shall you dance for the stars?
Shall you play with the sea?
Shall you swim like the whale?
Shall you follow the sun?
O Cushlamochree, has your dreaming begun?

Cariad Bach, O Cariad Bach,
Shall you sing to the moon?
Shall you shout for the dark?
Shall you whisper with bears?
Shall you waken the night?
O Cariad Bach, soft dreams and sleep tight.

*Cushlamochree is Gaelic for 'darling', and
Cariad Bach is Welsh for 'little darling'*

The Mother Moon

LOUISA MAY ALCOTT

The moon upon the wide sea
Placidly looks down,
Smiling with her mild face,
Though the ocean frown.
Clouds may dim her brightness,
But soon they pass away,
And she shines out, unaltered,
O'er the little waves at play.
So 'mid the storm or sunshine,
Wherever she may go,
Led on by her hidden power
The wild sea must plow.

As the tranquil evening moon
Looks on that restless sea,
So a mother's gentle face,
Little child, is watching thee.
Then banish every tempest,
Chase all your clouds away,
That smoothly and brightly
Your quiet heart may play.

Let cheerful looks and actions
Like shining ripples flow,
Following the mother's voice,
Singing as they go.

Morning Song

SARA TEASDALE

A diamond of a morning
Waked me an hour too soon;
Dawn had taken in the stars
And left the faint white moon.

O white moon, you are lonely,
It is the same with me,
But we have the world to roam over,
Only the lonely are free.

My Brilliant Image

HAFEZ

I wish I could show you
When you are lonely or in darkness,

The Astonishing Light
Of your own Being!

Index of first lines

A bee that was searching for sweets one day	180
a blind old lady with silver eyes	388
A boat sits on the very shallows	113
A bunch of Christmas Roses, dear,	339
A cheer for the snow – the drifting snow!	348
A clear waterfall;	110
A dash of spray;	122
A diamond of a morning	412
A fine and subtle spirit dwells	281
A flock of winds came winging from the North,	60
A granite rock in the mountain side	203
A green land full of rivers	111
A Light exists in Spring	11
A little bird woke singing in the night,	18
A little Brook, that babbled under grass,	117
A power is on the earth and in the air,	258
A radiance in the midnight sky	259
A ring around the moon…	385
A scallop shell, loosed by the lifting tide,	143
A society grows great when old men plant trees whose	285
A spirit is out to-night!	253
A toadstool comes up in a night, –	280
A track, a print, a paw.	349
A week ago I had a fire	249
A withered shamrock, yet to me 'tis fair	301
About the Shark, phlegmatical one,	137
Across the dunes, in the waning light,	376
Across the land came a magic word	58
After the earthquake shock or lighting dart	192
All along the backwater,	139
An emerald is as green as grass;	262
An olive fire's a lovely thing;	247
And suddenly the giants tired of play. –	67
As a quiet little seedling	314
At Christmas I no more desire a rose	328

"At my time of life," said the Dandelion, 84
At the old tribal squatting-place 101
Autumn evening – 183
Awake! for Morning in the Bowl of Night 10
'Bad world,' the newspapers print. 'Bad, bad world.' 170
Because of the silent snow, we are all hushed 358
Bend low again, night of summer stars. 404
Between the moon coming out 371
Black swallows swooping or gliding 355
Busy old fool, unruly sun, 24
Cauld blaws the wind frae east to west, 345
Clear moon 333
Cold is the night 384
"Come, little leaves," said the wind one day, 68
Come play with me; 296
Crouched cold in a cave 231
Cushlamochree, O Cushlamochree 409
Dark nights growing 402
Day opens its eyes: sky's pillowed with cloud. 158
De snow, de sleet, de lack o' heat, 323
Dis breeze is an air conditioner 77
dive deep beneath the waves of the Sulu Sea 97
Do you ask what the birds say? The sparrow, the dove, 65
Don't cry, Caterpillar 311
Earth has not anything to show more fair: 25
Enjoy the earth gently 177
Every branch big with it, 341
Every morn is the world made new. 8
Everyone suddenly burst out singing; 32
Fire in the window! flashes in the pane! 234
Fire leaps as steel and flint 237
Five little owls in an old elm tree, 375
For ages long, my people have been 226
From out the west, where darkling storm-clouds float, 126
From what flowering tree 276
Full fathom five thy father lies; 100
"Give the engines room, 264
Glad that I live am I; 37
Great, wide, beautiful, wonderful World, 90

Greedy little sparrow,	343
Goodbye, goodbye to Summer!	34
He clasps the crag with crooked hands;	74
He who binds to himself a joy	33
Her grandfather always said	313
High up in the apple tree climbing I go,	199
How can one sell the air	75
How clear, how lovely bright,	21
How doth the little crocodile	129
How should I not be glad to contemplate	22
How still it is here in the woods. The trees	206
Hurt no living thing:	316
I am dotted silver threads dropped from heaven	118
I am the sea, I have something to say	218
I can remember	92
I can't hear the barista	298
I come from a distant land	214
I had a boat, and the boat had wings;	398
I must go down to the seas again, to the lonely sea and the sky,	159
I saw a star slide down the sky,	235
I saw the civil sun drying earth's tears –	365
I saw you toss the kites on high	73
I see people riding on shrieking horses,	260
I shall die hidden in a hut	59
I sing	216
I sometimes think I'd rather crow	306
I stood beside a hill	337
I told the Sun that I was glad,	16
I wandered lonely as a cloud	50
I was up way past my bedtime	318
I went to the Animal Fair	293
I will think as thinks the rabbit…	89
I wish I could show you	413
I wish I were a jelly fish	287
I'd rather listen to the winds voicing	64
If I were a rose	279
If woolly fleeces deck the heavenly way	12
If you asked what The Moon is	372

If you sit down at set of sun   36

If you were an owl   392

In a milkweed cradle   86

In Ancient Greece   307

In grows the gloaming,   196

In the Arctic summer   362

In the far corner   290

In the gloom of whiteness,   366

In the other gardens   263

In the small time   43

In the winter time we go   332

It hain't no use to grumble and complane;   128

It is a sultry day; the sun has drunk   87

It was a grey old day, it looked like rain   162

January brings the snow,   224

Lark-bird, lark-bird soaring high,   71

Leaves return to trees,   179

Lend me your ears now   146

Let's say that one evening   85

Listen...   382

Live thy Life,   200

Look at the stars! look, look up at the skies!   399

Love is the swamp we drove to today.   201

Mackerel sky, mackerel sky...   127

March winds bring April showers   70

Monday I found a boot –   130

My candle burns at both ends;   250

My heart's in the Highlands, my heart is not here,   215

My niece believes all animals   294

'Never,' said my father,   304

Night comes   406

Now, once upon a time, a nest of fairies   188

Nymph, nymph, what are your beads?   207

"O dandelion, yellow as gold,   288

O white little lights at Carney's Point,   251

Of all the plants   295

Oh! hush thee, my baby, the night is behind us,   378

Oh! I have slipped the surly bonds of Earth   23

Oh! let it rest;   408

418

Oh, the beautiful snow!	338
Oh, the noise of Piccadilly – its rumble and its roar!	377
Oh, where do you come from,	144
On the hard crest of a snowdrift,	344
Once I saw a little bird	83
Out of us all	54
Picture a vacuum	28
Professor Snow has hair of white	352
Rain on the high prairies,	125
Red sky at night, shepherd's delight	257
Right here on this bench a city idiot (me)	291
Rose dreamed she was a lily,	310
Rustily creak the crickets: Jack Frost came down last night,	351
Said the Wind to the Moon, "I will blow you out;	393
See lightening is flashing,	72
Shall I dwell in my shell?	278
Slipping softly through the sky	400
Slowly the fog,	391
Snow has scattered, returning green to the fields	195
Some of it is brown	222
Some say the world will end in fire,	233
Something told the wild geese	357
Soon as the sun forsook the eastern main	30
Soon,	7
Spring's	317
Sun sets Friday, clear as bell	13
Tall nettles cover up, as they have done	286
That is rain on dry ground. We heard it:	108
The day has eyes.	374
The earth is motionless	212
The earth, they say,	169
The Earthquake rumbled	205
The evening is coming,	389
The forest drips and glows with green.	232
The Frost performs its secret ministry,	364
The Microbe is so very small	297
The moon has a face like the clock in the hall;	407
The moon upon the wide sea	410

The night is darkening round me,   386

The night is white,   397

the old world began   208

the ocean turns green algae into light,   152

The people could fly –   26

The quiet snow   356

The rooks are building on the trees;   17

The rustling of leaves under the feet in woods
and under hedges;   178

The same stream of life that runs through my
veins night and day   275

The sea is calm tonight.   160

THE SEA! the sea! the open sea!   151

The snowflakes are falling   340

The south wind brings wet weather;   66

The spring is coming! hear it blow!   14

The stars must make an awful noise   20

The sun descending in the west,   379

The sun that brief December day   327

The tide rises, the tide falls,   138

The tiny fish enjoy themselves   124

The two worlds collided   182

The way a crow   336

The whole city has come out to see the river   360

The whole street would exhale   342

The wind rippled an armour's chainmail in the water,   334

The wind stooped down and wrote a sweet, small word,   359

The woodpecker pecked out a little round hole   121

There is pleasure in the pathless woods   76

There was a little guinea pig,   312

There will be thunder then. Remember me.   246

There's no smoke in the chimney,   132

There's something truly magical   141

They shut the road through the woods   193

They went to sea in a Sieve, they did,   153

This is how the wind shifts: 78

This life that we call our own   244

This morning the sun   5

This ray of sun I claim   38

'Tis the last rose of summer   277

Two old crows sat on a fence rail.   52

Tyger Tyger, burning bright,   242

Until I saw the sea   115

Upon the mountain's distant head,   213

We built each   239

We have a little garden,   284

We sat within the farm-house old,   254

We walk through the woods near my house   184

We were twinshoots sprouting beautifully on a tree.   289

What does the feather say to the grass?   309

What is this life if, full of care,   31

What way does the wind come? What way does he go?   80

When I consider everything that grows   308

When I was eight years old   189

When I was twelve   325

When the earth is turned in spring   174

When the sea has devoured the ships,   245

When the shadow of a tree is curved,   187

When the world turns completely upside down   329

When you walk through a storm   91

Where all the trees bear golden flowers,   261

White sheep, white sheep,   49

Wide sleeves sway.   136

Wild harmattan winds whip you   79

With solid drops the hail that showers down   346

With the wasp at the innermost heart of a peach,   302

Within this black hive to-night   387

Who has seen the wind?   57

Whose woods these are I think I know.   347

Woke up this morning   46

Wynken, Blynken, and Nod one night   133

You cannot put a fire out;   236

You say, "Welcome in, Air   61

You spotted snakes with double tongue,   383

421

Index of poets

Agard, John 317
Akhmatova, Anna 246, 344
Al-Aadiyya, Mahd 260
Alcott, Louisa May 410
Allingham, William 34
Alma-Tadema, Laurence 71
Alvi, Moniza 309
Anonymous 12, 13, 49, 66, 70, 83, 86, 92, 127, 179, 257, 285, 288, 293, 306, 310, 312, 333, 338, 343, 374, 375, 384, 385
Anouka, Jade 141
Antrobus, Raymond 298
ar-Rumaikiyya, Itimad 334
Arnold, Matthew 160
Arshi, Mona 239
Atta, Dean 294, 318
Bashir, Hafsah Aneela 237
Bashō, Matsuo 110, 183, 276
Belloc, Hilaire 297
Bergengren, Ralph 174
bint Bahdal, Maysun 64
bint Khalid al-Bahiliyya, Safiyya 289
Bishop, Elizabeth 67
Blake, William 33, 242, 379
Bloom, Valerie 77, 323
Bridges, Robert 335
Brontë, Anne 281
Brontë, Emily 386
Brown, George Mackay 130
Brown, Paul Cameron 113
Browne, Jane Euphemia 17, 144
Brownlee, Liz 362
Bryant, William Cullen 87, 213, 258
Burns, Robert 215, 345

Byron, Lord 176
Carroll, Lewis 129
Cawein, Madison Julius 14
Chesterton, G. K. 287
Chief Seattle 75
Chitrakar, Joydeb and Moyna 146
Clare, John 178
Coats, Lucy 409
Coleridge, Mary 132, 398
Coleridge, Samuel Taylor 65, 364
Coleridge, Sara 72, 224
Cook, Eliza 348
Coolidge, Susan 8, 192
Cooper, George 68
Cornwall, Barry 150
Crapsey, Adelaide 382
Davies, William Henry 31, 249
Davis, Jack 182
de Regniers, Beatrice Schenk 406
Dharker, Imtiaz 304, 360
Dickinson, Emily 11, 236
Dodge, Mary Mapes 234, 392
Donne, John 24
Drake, Nick 325
Drinkwater, John 16
Dunbar, Paul Laurence 180, 314
Dunbar-Nelson, Alice Moore 251
Eliot, George (Mary Ann Evans) 36
Ewing, Juliana Horatia 84, 117
Field, Eugene 133
Field, Rachel 357
Fisher, Aileen 169
flanagan, oakley 170
Fletcher, John Gould 355
Foott, Mary Hannay 259

Freeman, Mary E. Wilkins	188
Frost, Robert	233, 336, 347
Fry, Christopher	108
Gibran, Khalil	118
Gill, Marjorie Lotfi	313
Godden, Salena	352, 388
Grahame, Kenneth	139
Greek Proverb	285
Greenwell, Dora	302
Hafez	413
Hamid, Triska	38
Hammerstein, Oscar II	91
Hardy, Thomas	341
Harrold, A. F.	222
Hartmann, Sadakichi	376
Hensley, Sophie M.	122
Herford, Oliver	205
Holley, Marietta	253
Hood, Thomas	389
Hopkins, Gerard Manley	399
Horace	195
Housman, A. E.	21
Inchfawn, Fay	58
Jackson, Leroy F.	340
Jewett, Sophie	261
Johnson, Emily Pauline	126
Khafajah, Ibn	346
Khayyam, Omar	10
Kipling, Rudyard	193, 378
Kisuule, Vanessa	342
Knister, Raymond	356
Lampman, Archibald	206
Lawrence, D. H.	124, 358
Lawson, Lizzie	339
Lear, Edward	153
Lee, Iona	196
Lesson, Luka	307
Lightbown, Stephen	184
Lindsay, Vachel	52, 264
Longfellow, Henry Wadsworth	138, 254
Lowell, Amy	199, 400
Luxx, Lisa	61
MacDonald, George	89, 393
Mackellar, Dorothea	244
Maclean, Kate Seymour	18
Magee, John Gillespie	23
Mahfouz, Sabrina	111, 218, 279, 349
Mahon, Derek	22
Masefield, John	159
Masters, Edgar Lee	245
McCreary, F. R.	391
McNish, Hollie	189
Melville, Herman	137
Mew, Charlotte	408
Meynell, Alice	60
Millay, Edna St. Vincent	175, 250
Mitchell, Adrian	208
Mole, Simon	97
Monro, Harold	20, 207
Moore, Lilian	115
Moore, Thomas	277
Mordecai, Pamela C.	5
Moreland, John Richard	397
Morgan, Michaela	231
Morgenstern, Christian	278
Moskowitz, Cheryl	402
Naderi, Partaw	214
Nichols, Grace	26, 311
Nikyu	371
Noonuccal, Oodgeroo (Kath Walker)	101
Osman, Hibaq	372
Osundare, Niyi	216
Parkes, Nii Ayikwei	79
Pembroke, Nora	301
Piper, Edwin Ford	125

Potter, Beatrix 284

Pratyusha 152

Quessep, Giovanni 85

Quraishi, Shazea 158

Randall, Talia 291

Rands, William Brighty 90

Reed, Helen Leah 377

Reese, Lizette Woodworth 37, 359

Ridge, Lola 212

Riley, James Whitcomb 128, 405

Roberts, Elizabeth Madox 121

Rodger, Deanna 201

Rossetti, Christina 57, 262, 280, 316

Rudd-Mitchell, David 7

Sandburg, Carl 404

Sassoon, Siegfried 32

Service, Robert William 247

Shakespeare, William 100, 308, 328, 383

Sigerson Shorter, Dora 143

Smith, Alan 46

Stephens, James 332

Stevens, Wallace 78

Stevenson, Robert Louis 73, 263, 407

Tagore, Rabindranath 275

Taylor, Joelle 43

Teasdale, Sara 235, 337, 412

Tempest, Kate 28, 162

Tennyson, Alfred, Lord 74, 200

Thaxter, Celia 351

Thomas, Edward 54, 286, 366

Thoreau, Henry David 365

Toomer, Jean 387

Walker, Bertrand N.O. 226

Wei, Wang 116

West African Proverb 187

Wheatley, Phillis 30

Whittier, John Greenleaf 327

Wilcox, Ella Wheeler 203

Wolfe, Humbert 290

Wordsworth, Dorothy 80

Wordsworth, William 25

Wordsworth, William and Mary 50

Wright, Judith 232

Wylie, Elinor 59, 329

Yang Kuei-Fei 136

Yeats, W.B. 296

Acknowledgements

The compiler and publisher would like to thank the following for permission to use copyright material –

Agard, John, 'The Little Green Man Addresses a Leaf', from *The Coming of the Little Green Man* (Bloodaxe Books, 2019) © John Agard, 2019. Reproduced with permission of Bloodaxe Books. www.bloodaxebooks.com. **Akhmatova, Anna,** 'On the Hard Crust' and 'Thunder' by Anna Akhatova © trans A.S Kline, first published on Poetsofmodernity.xyz. Reproduced by the permission of the translator. **al-Aadiyya, Mahd,** 'Flame Life', from *Classical Poems by Arab Women: A Bilingual Anthology* (1999) © trans from the Arabic by Abdullah Al-Udhari. Reproduced with kind permission of Saqi Books. **Alvi, Moniza,** 'A Soft White Feather Lying on the Grass', from *Blackbird, Bye Bye* (Bloodaxe Books, 2018) © Moniza Alvi. Reproduced with permission of Bloodaxe Books. www.bloodaxebooks.com. **Anouka, Jade,** 'A Beach on a Foggy Day' © Jade Anouka, 2019. **Antrobus, Raymond,** 'With Birds You're Never Lonely' © Raymond Antrobus, 2019. **Arshi, Mona,** 'Paper' © Mona Arshi, 2019. **Atta, Dean,** 'How Pigeons Growl' and 'Shuffle Monster' © Dean Atta, 2019. **Bashir, Hafsah Aneela,** 'We The Fire Crowned Flares' © Hafsah Aneela Bashir, 2019. **Belloc, Hilaire,** 'The Microbe' from *More Beasts for Worse Children* by Hilaire Belloc reprinted by permission of Peters Fraser & Dunlop (www.petersfraserdunlop.com) on behalf of the Estate of Hilaire Belloc. **bint Bahdal, Maysun,** 'Wallcracks' by Maysun bint Bahdal, from *Classical Poems by Arab Women: A Bilingual Anthology* (1999) © trans from the Arabic by Abdullah Al-Udhari. Reproduced with kind permission of Saqi Books. **bint Khalid al-Bahiliyya, Safiyya,** 'Twinshoots', from *Classical Poems by Arab Women: A Bilingual Anthology* (1999) © trans from the Arabic by Abdullah Al-Udhari. Reproduced with kind permission of Saqi Books. **Bloom, Valerie,** 'De' and 'Dis Breeze' © Valerie Bloom, from *Let Me Touch the Sky* (2000). Reprinted by permission of Eddison Pearson Ltd on behalf of Valerie Bloom. **Brown, George Mackay,** 'Beachcomber' © George Mackay Brown. Reproduced by permission of John Murray Press, a division of Hodder and Stoughton Limited. **Chitrakar, Joydeb and Moyna,** 'Tsunami' Text by Joydeb and Moyna Chitrakar. Translated from the Bengali by Mala Chakraborthy and Sirish Rao. Original Edition © Tara Books Pvt Ltd, Chennai, India. www.tarabooks.com **Coats, Lucy,** 'Cushlamochree', first published in *One Hungry Baby* (Orchard Books, 1992) © Lucy Coats. Reproduced by permission of the author. **Brownlee, Liz,** 'Snow Fox', first published in *Poetry for a Change* (Otter-Barry, 2018) © Liz Brownlee. Reproduced by permission of the author. **de Regniers, Beatrice Schenk,** 'Night Comes', from *A Bunch of Poems and Verses* (1977) © Beatrice Schenk de Regniers. Copyright Renewed and Reserved. Used by permission of Marian Reiner. **Dharker, Imtiaz,** 'How to Cut a Pomegranate', from *The Terrorist at my Table* (Bloodaxe Books, 2006) and 'The Elephant is Walking on the River Thames' from *Luck is the Hook* (Bloodaxe Books, 2018) © Imtiaz Dharker. Reproduced with permission of Bloodaxe Books. www.bloodaxebooks.com. **Drake, Nick,** 'The Farewell Glacier', from *The Farewell Glacier* (Bloodaxe Books, 2012) © Nick Drake. Reproduced with permission of Bloodaxe Books. www.bloodaxebooks.com.

428

Quessep, Giovanni, 'Someone Is Saved by Listening to the Nightingale', from *A Greek Verse for Ophelia and Other Poems* (2018) © Giovanni Quessep. Trans from the Spanish © Felipe Quintama and Ranald Barnicot, 2018. Reproduced with kind permission of Out-Spoken Press. **Quraishi, Shazea,** 'Ghazal with Rain and Birds' © Shazea Quraishi, 2019. **Randall, Talia,** 'Nature Poem' © Talia Randall, 2019. **Rodger, Deanna,** 'Love is This Swamp' © Deanna Rodger 2019. **Rudd-Mitchell, David,** 'Chorus', from *Diversifly* (2018) © David Rudd-Mitchell. Reproduced by kind permission of Fair Acre Press. **Smith, Alan,** 'Emily Hurricane', first published in *Under the Moon and Over the Sea: A Collection of Caribbean Poems* (Candlewick Press, 2002) © Alan Smith. Reproduced by permission of the author. **Taylor, Joelle,** 'Legend of the First Wind' © Joelle Taylor, 2019. **Tempest, Kate,** 'Picture a Vacuum' written by Kate Tempest. Courtesy of Domino Publishing Company Limited, and 'Puddle' © Kate Tempest, 2019. **Wright, Judith,** 'Rainforest', from *Collected Poems* (1994) © Judith Wright, the words reproduced by kind permission of HarperCollins Australia and New Zealand.

Every effort has been made to clear copyright. Should there be any inadvertent omission please apply to the publisher for rectification.

Amnesty International endorses this collection because its poets express, with great power and beauty, why we all need a clean, healthy and sustainable planet if we are to be safe and to flourish.

Amnesty International is the world's leading human rights organisation. We educate, we campaign for justice and we work to protect people wherever fairness, equality, truth and dignity are denied.

We vigorously oppose climate change because it will have a devastating impact on people's rights everywhere and we support other organisations that are also working towards the same goals.

You can find out more about Amnesty International on our website – most of our content is written for an adult readership, but we also have resources for younger activists.

If you would like to know more about climate change and how you can get involved, you might be interested in the organisations below. If you are a younger reader, please ask an adult to supervise your research to help you find the most appropriate materials.

Greenpeace
Friends of the Earth
Extinction Rebellion
Fridays For Future
350.org

THIS BOOK IS ENDORSED BY
AMNESTY INTERNATIONAL